THE PLATONIC SOLIDS

COLORING BOOK

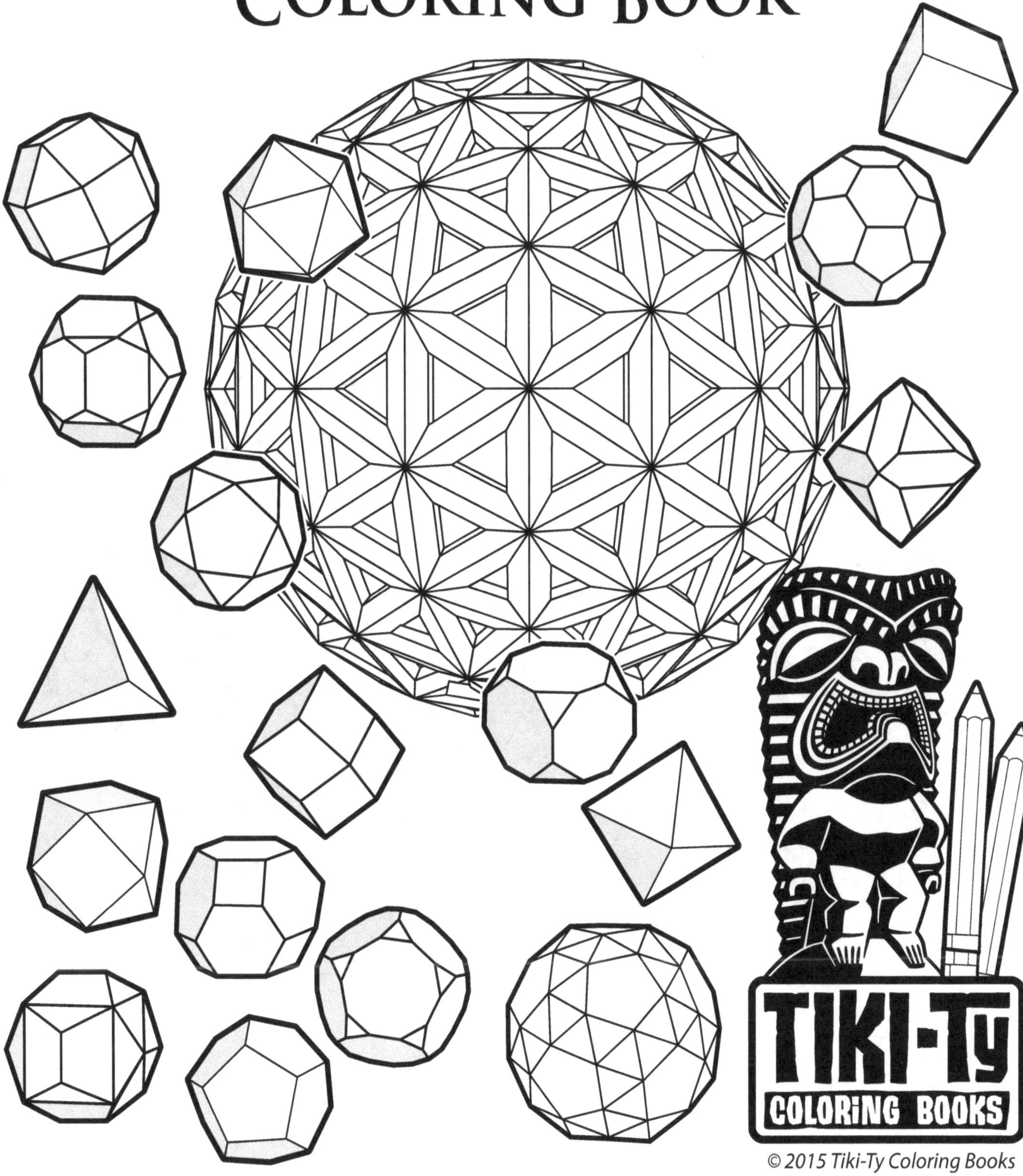

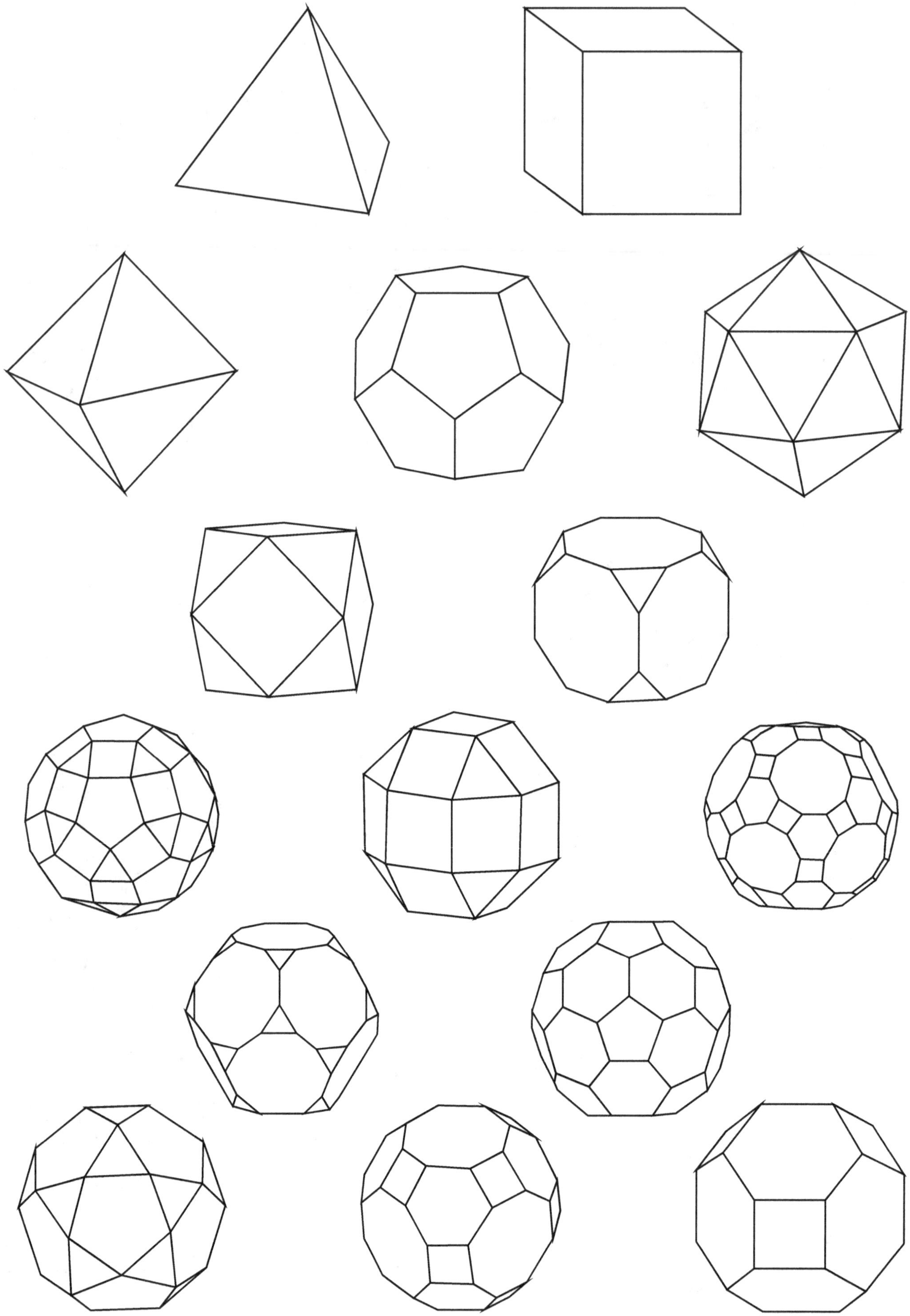

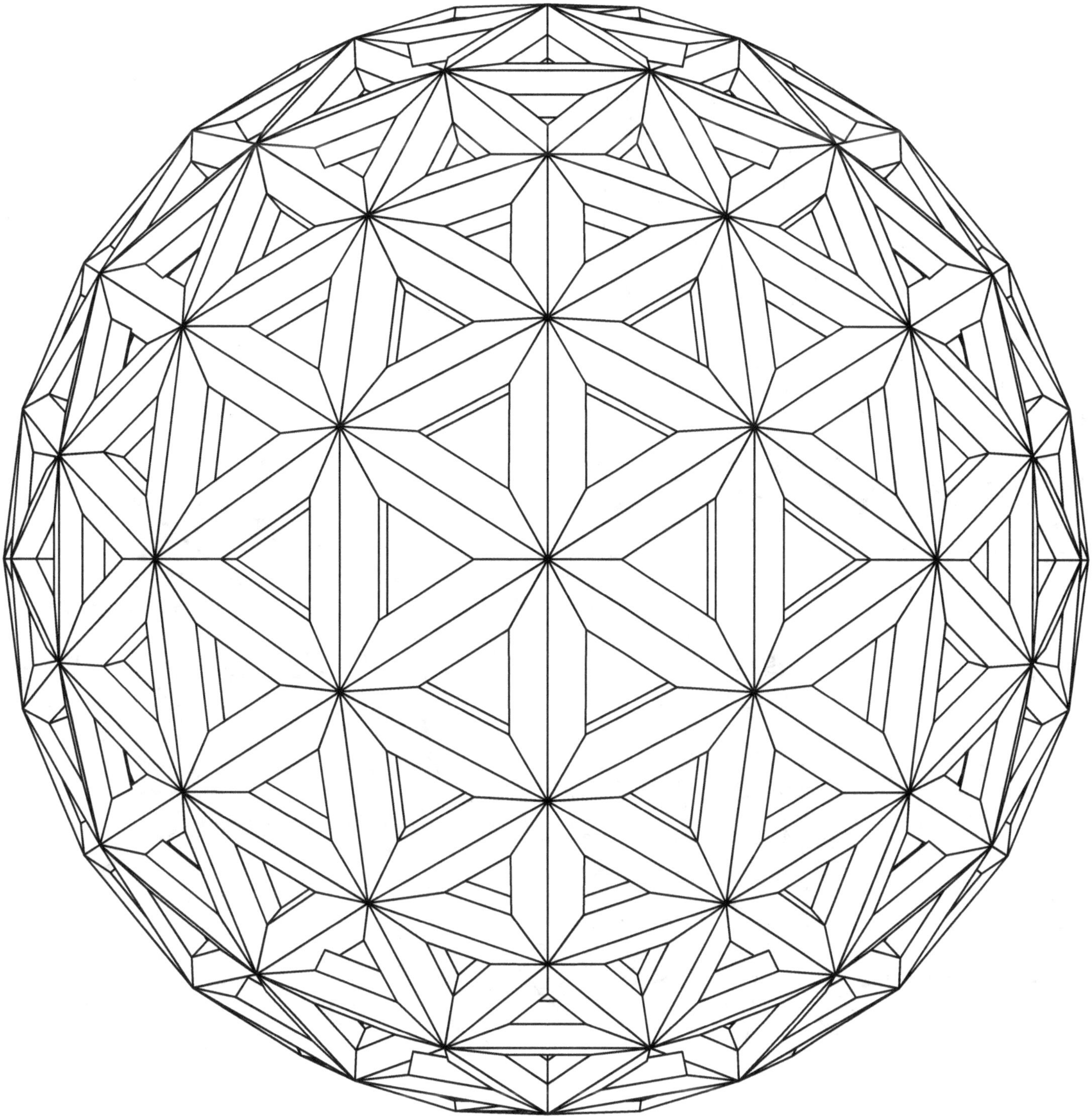

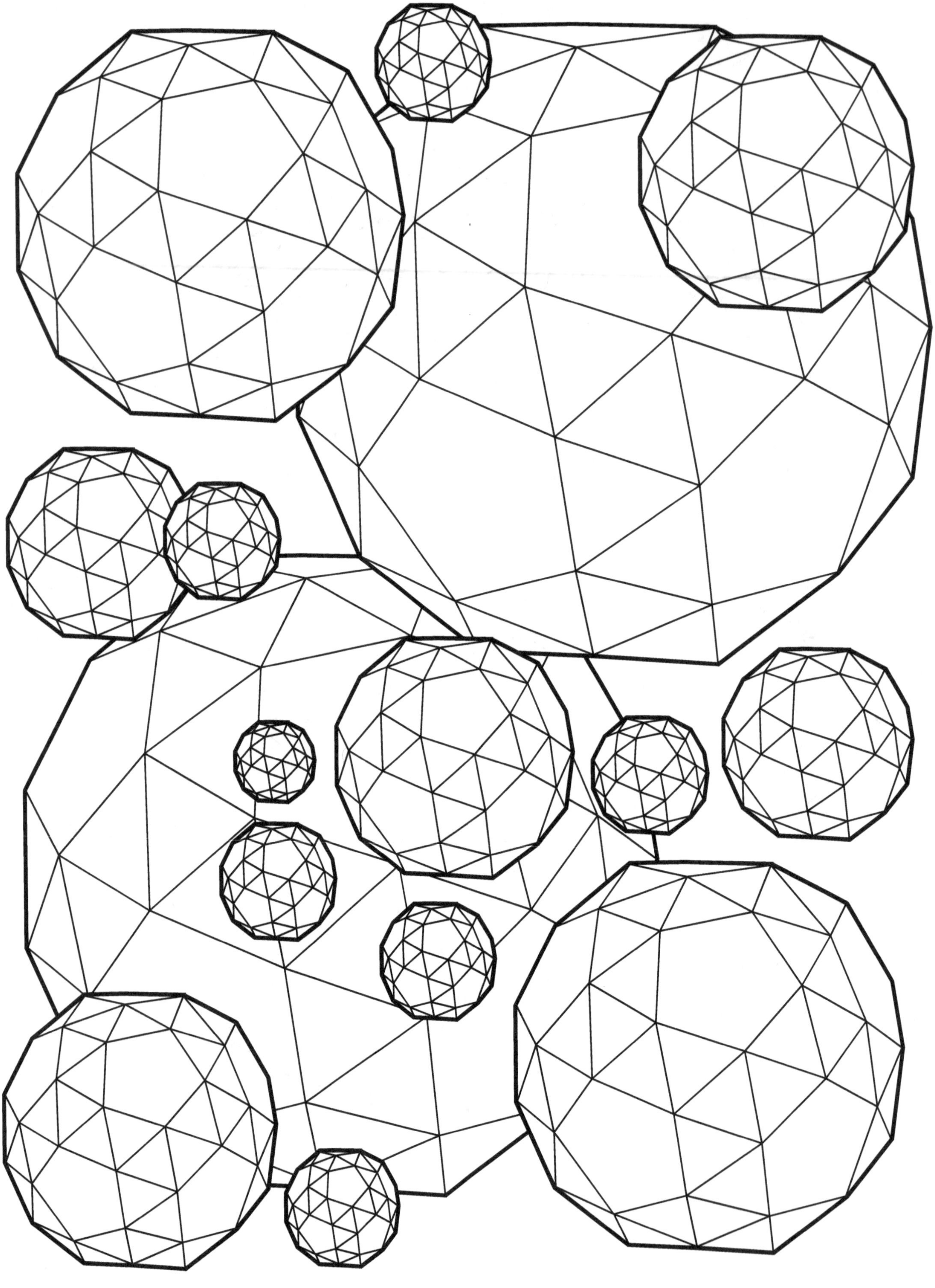

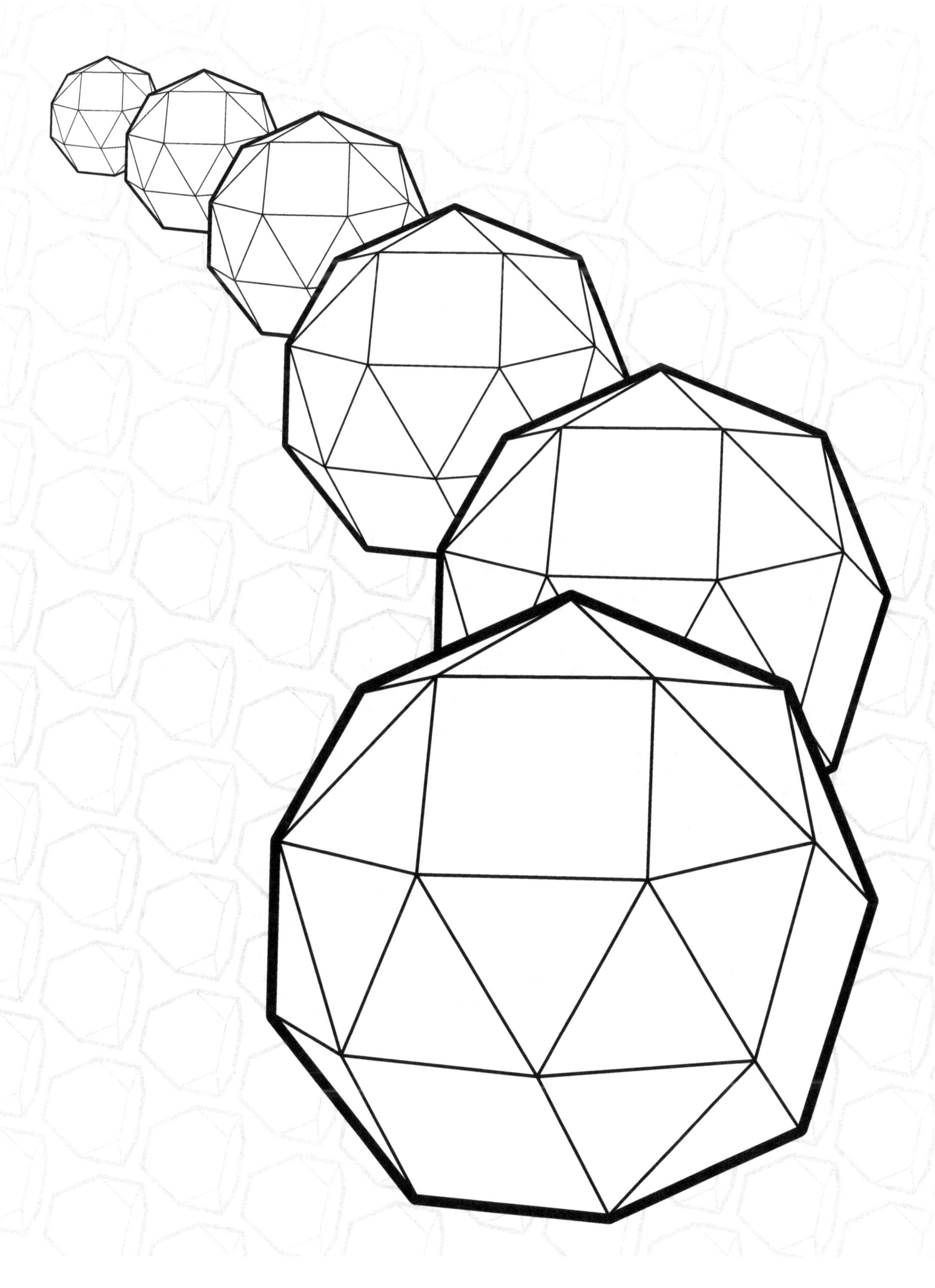

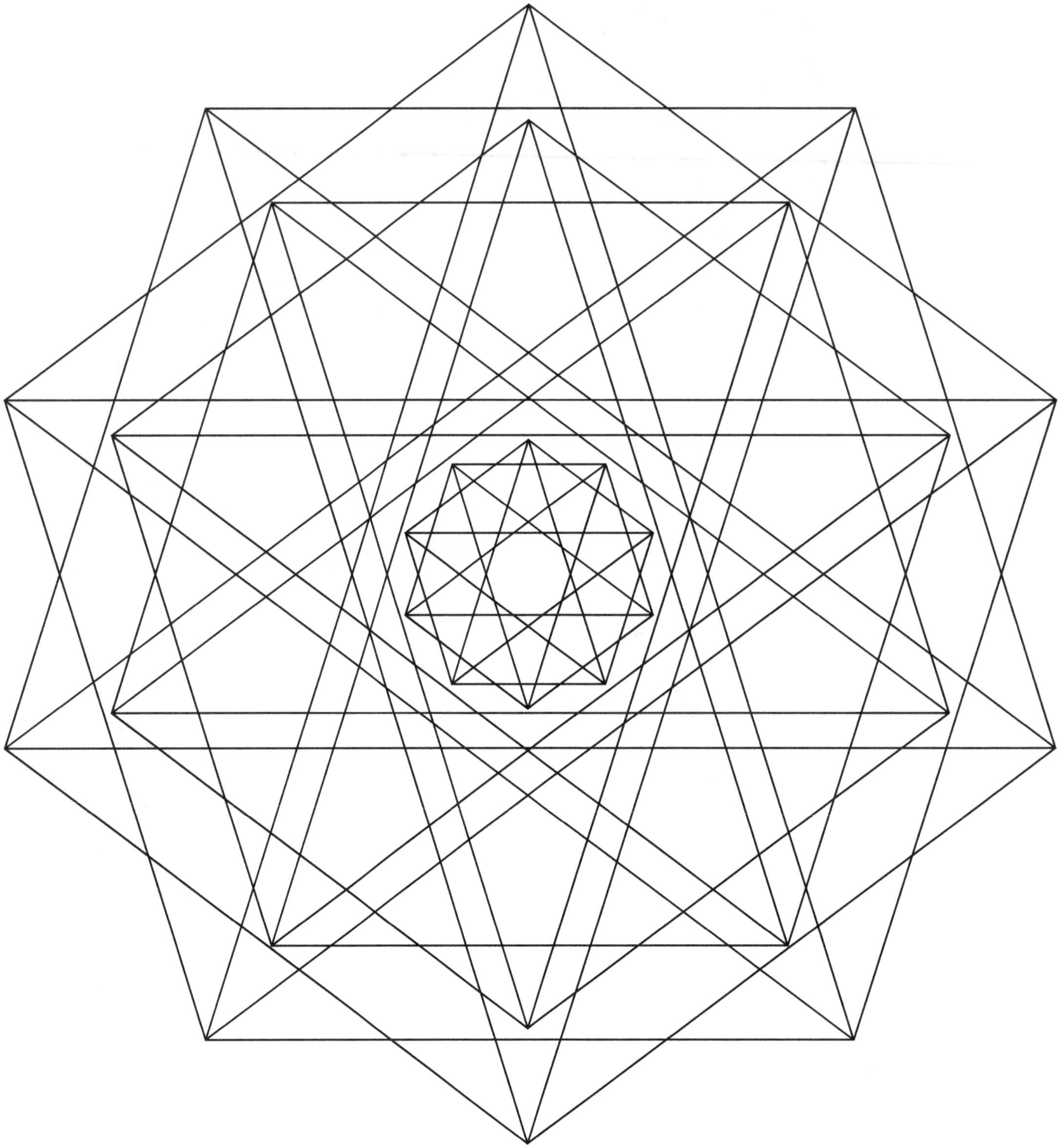

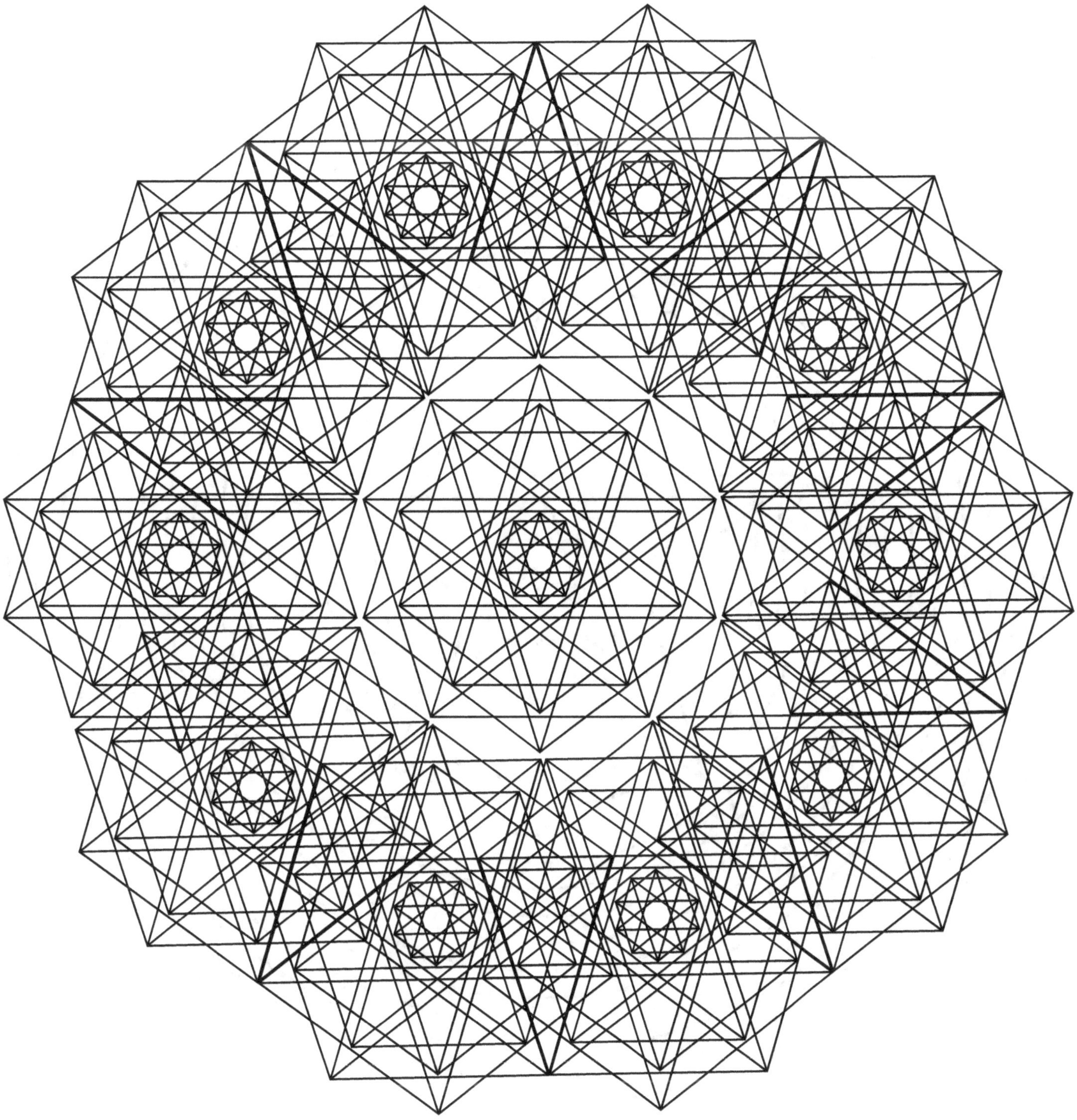

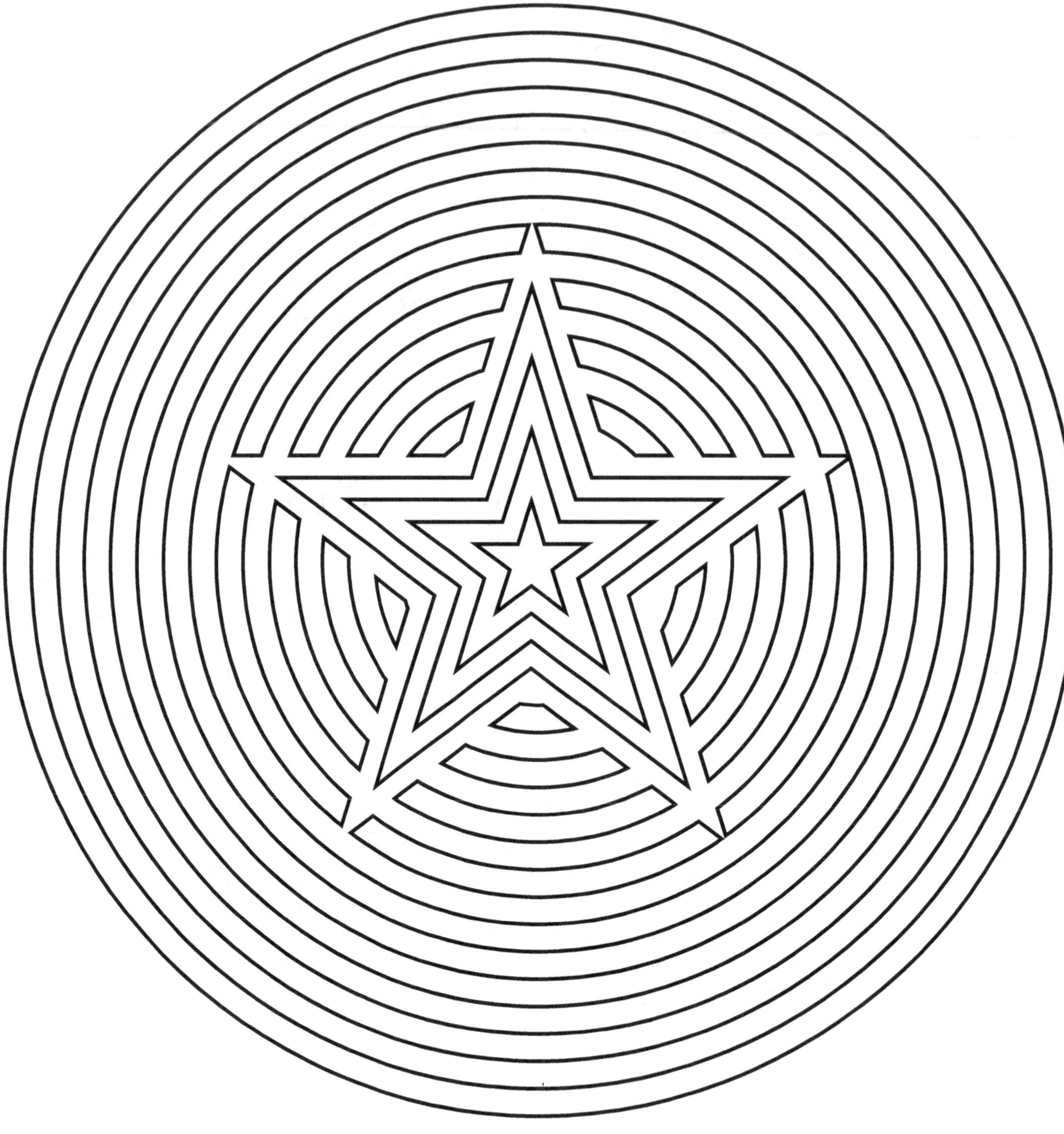

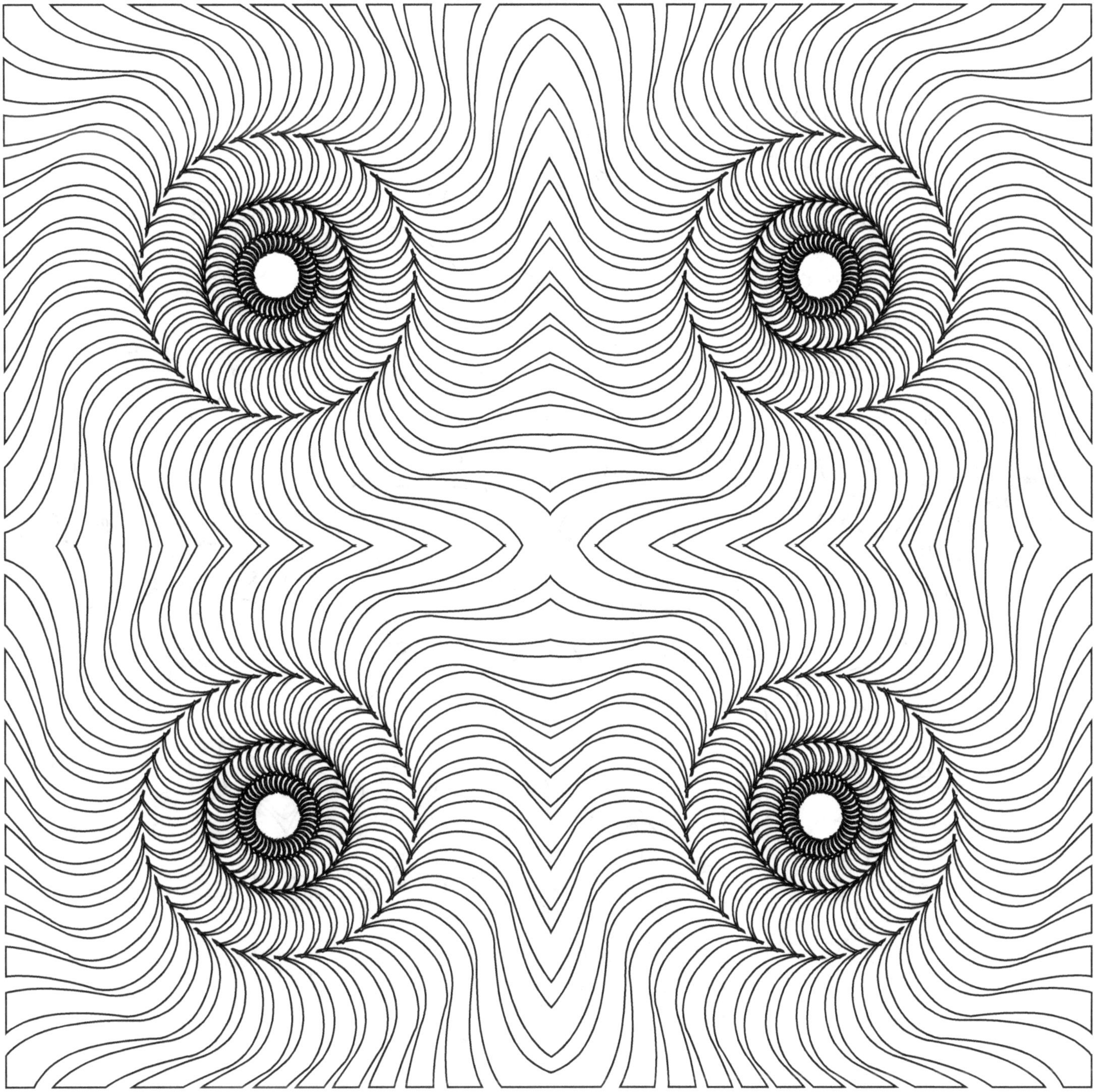

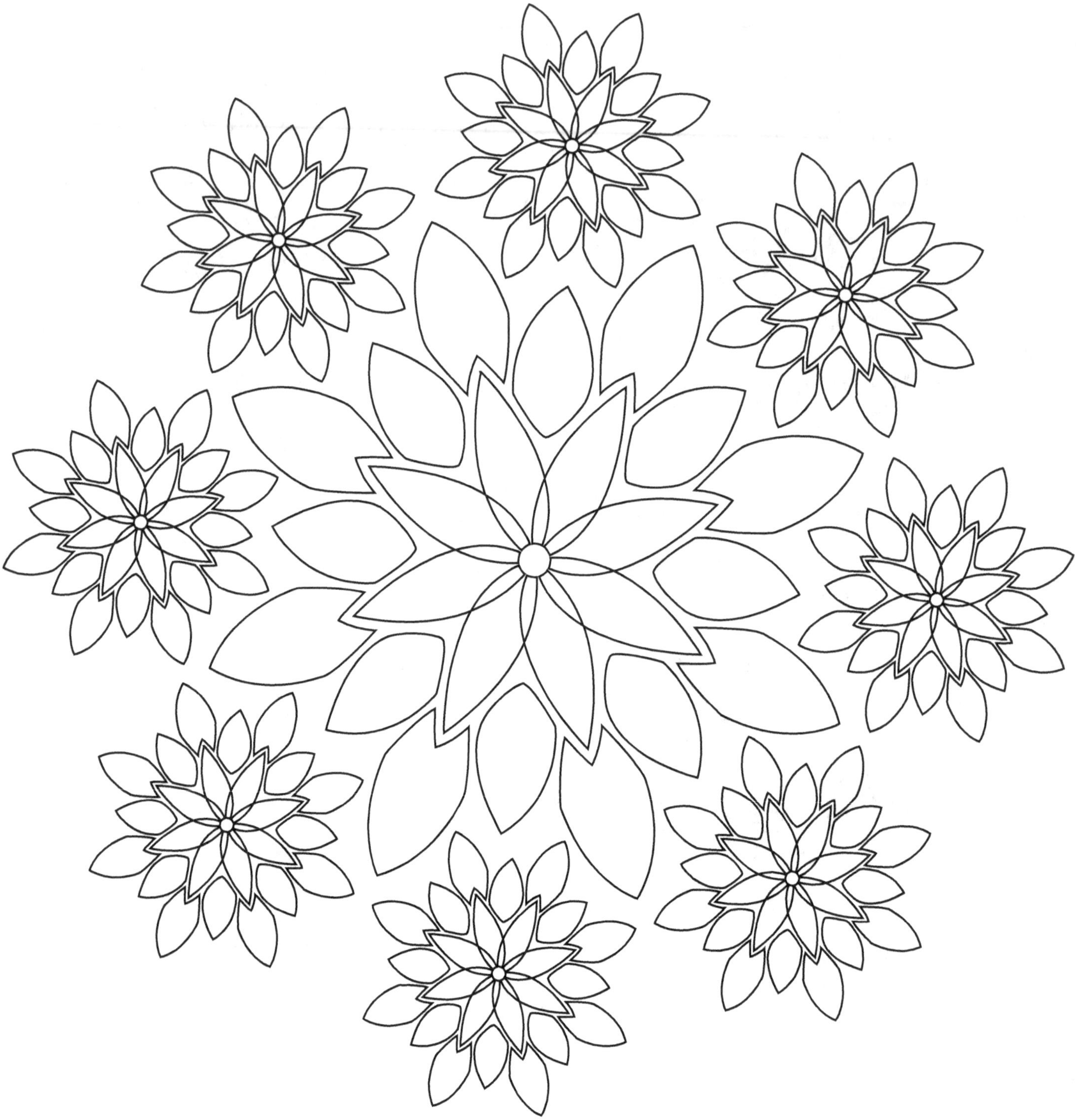

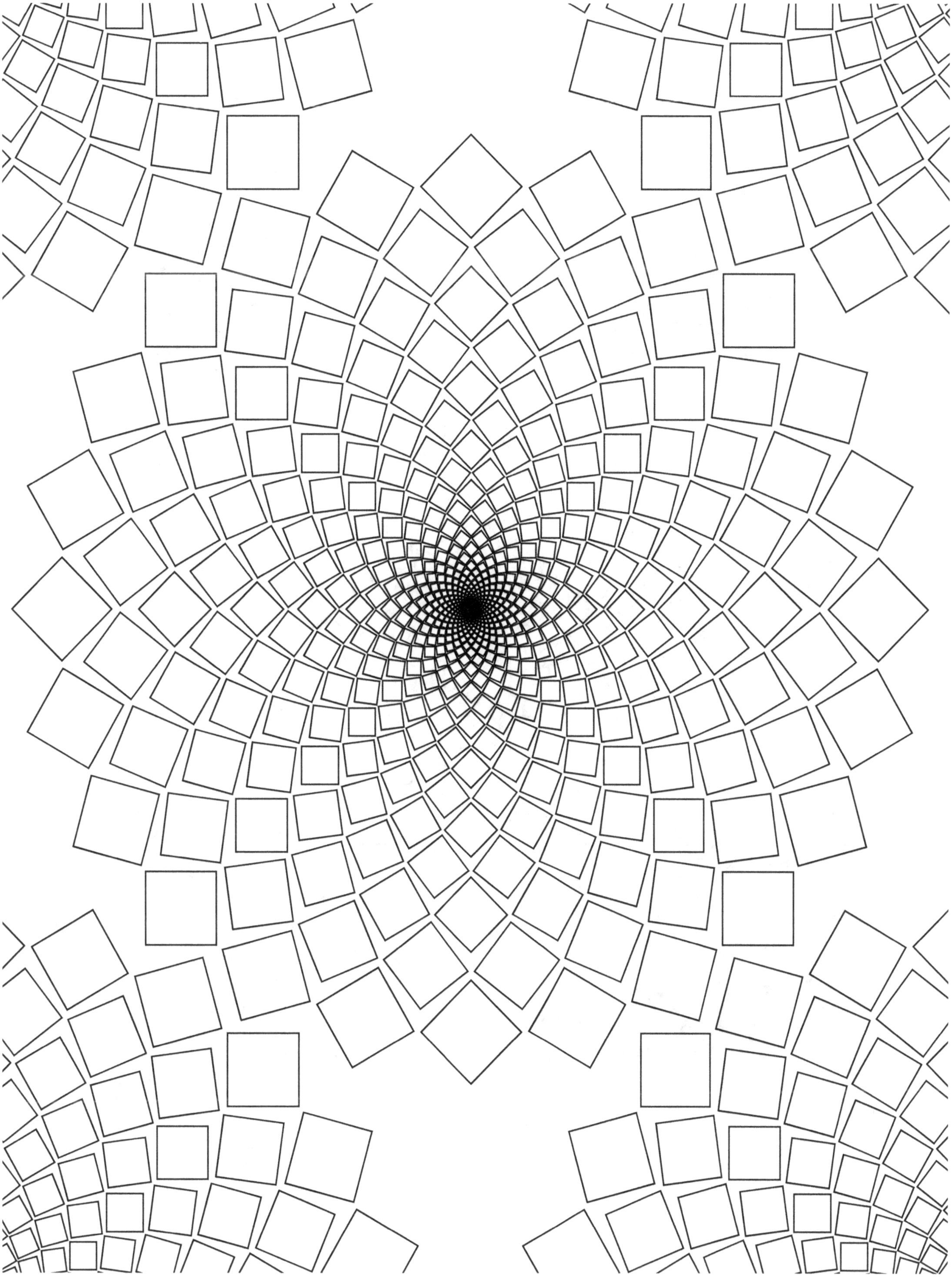

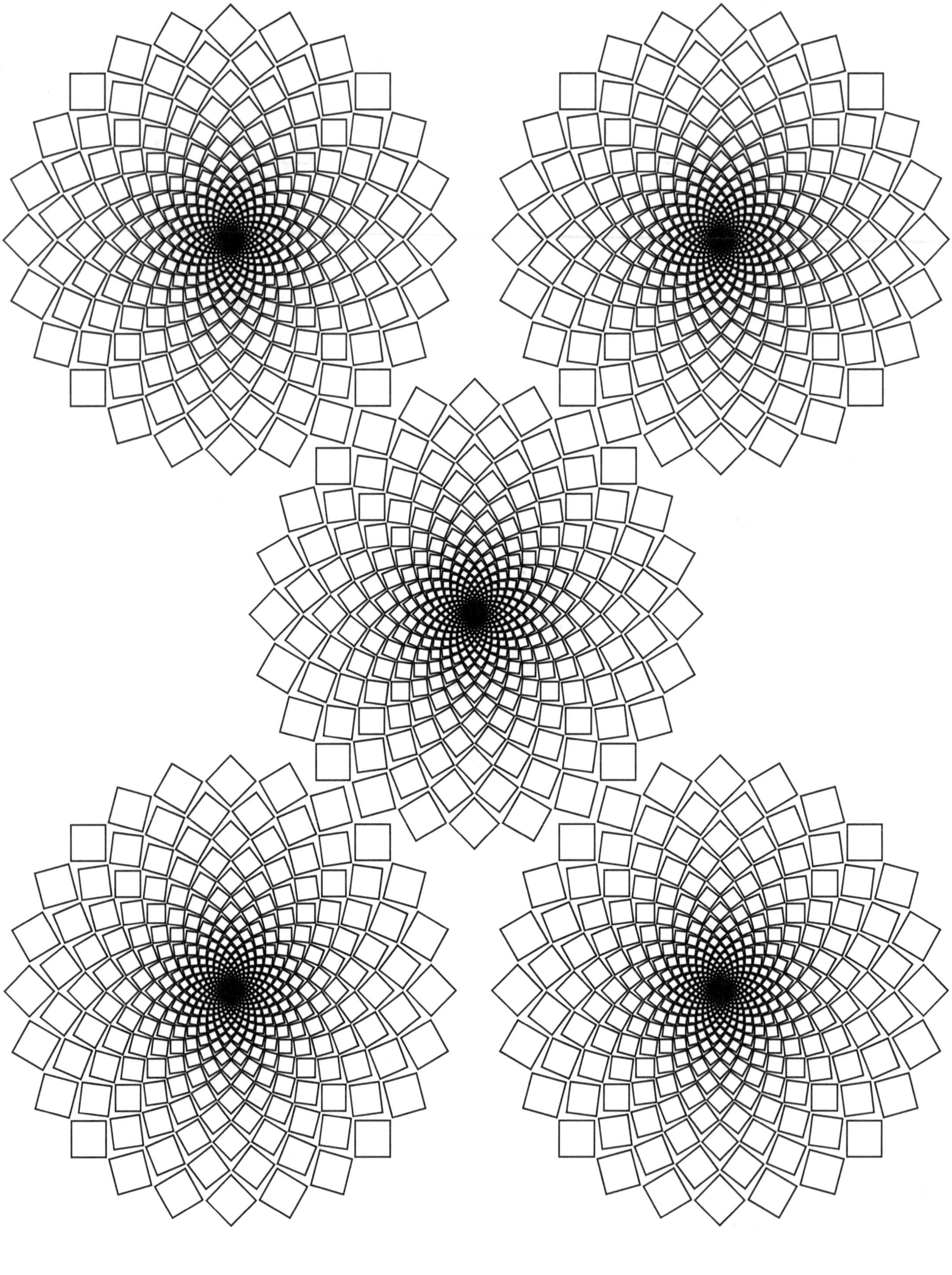

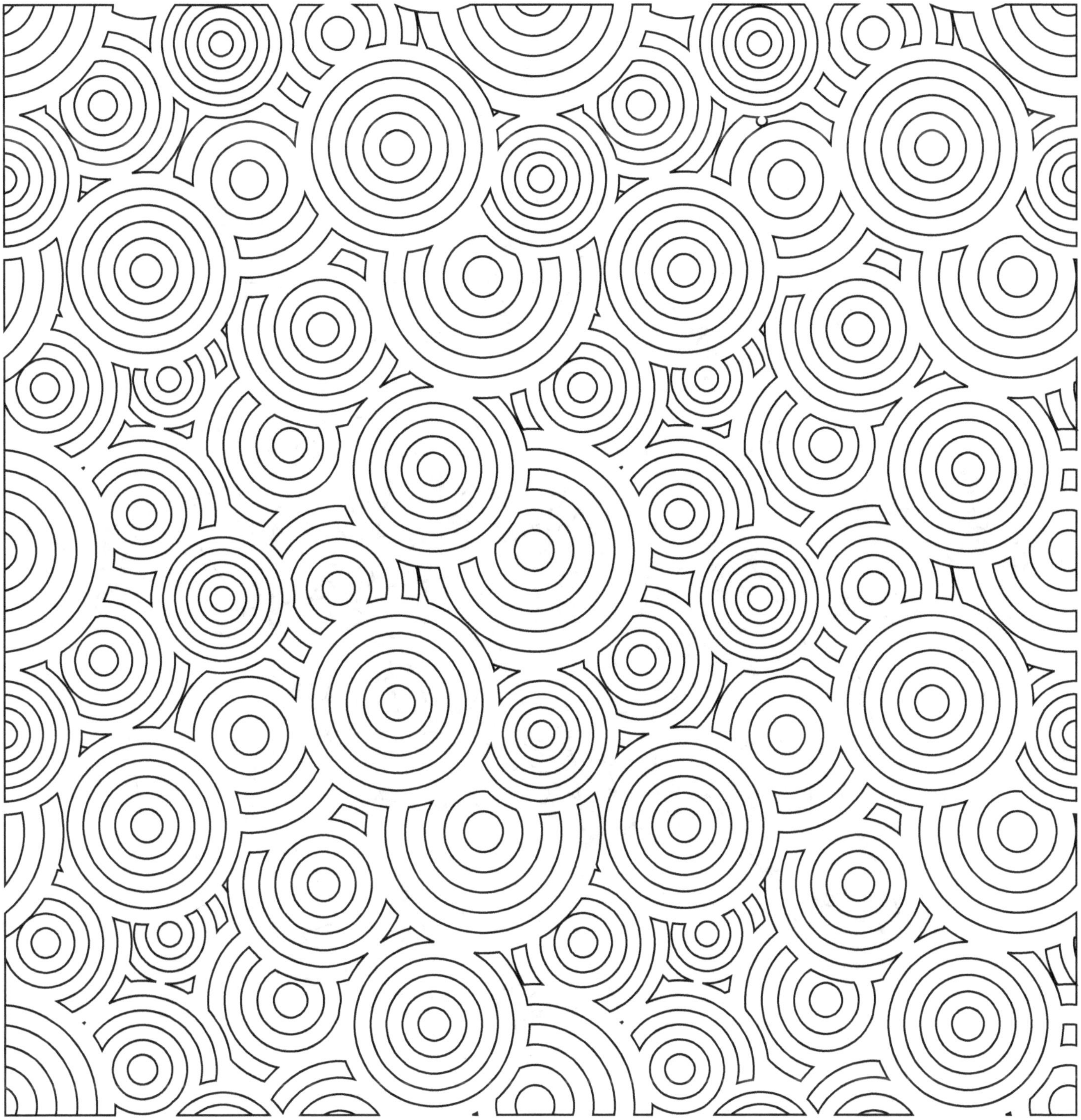

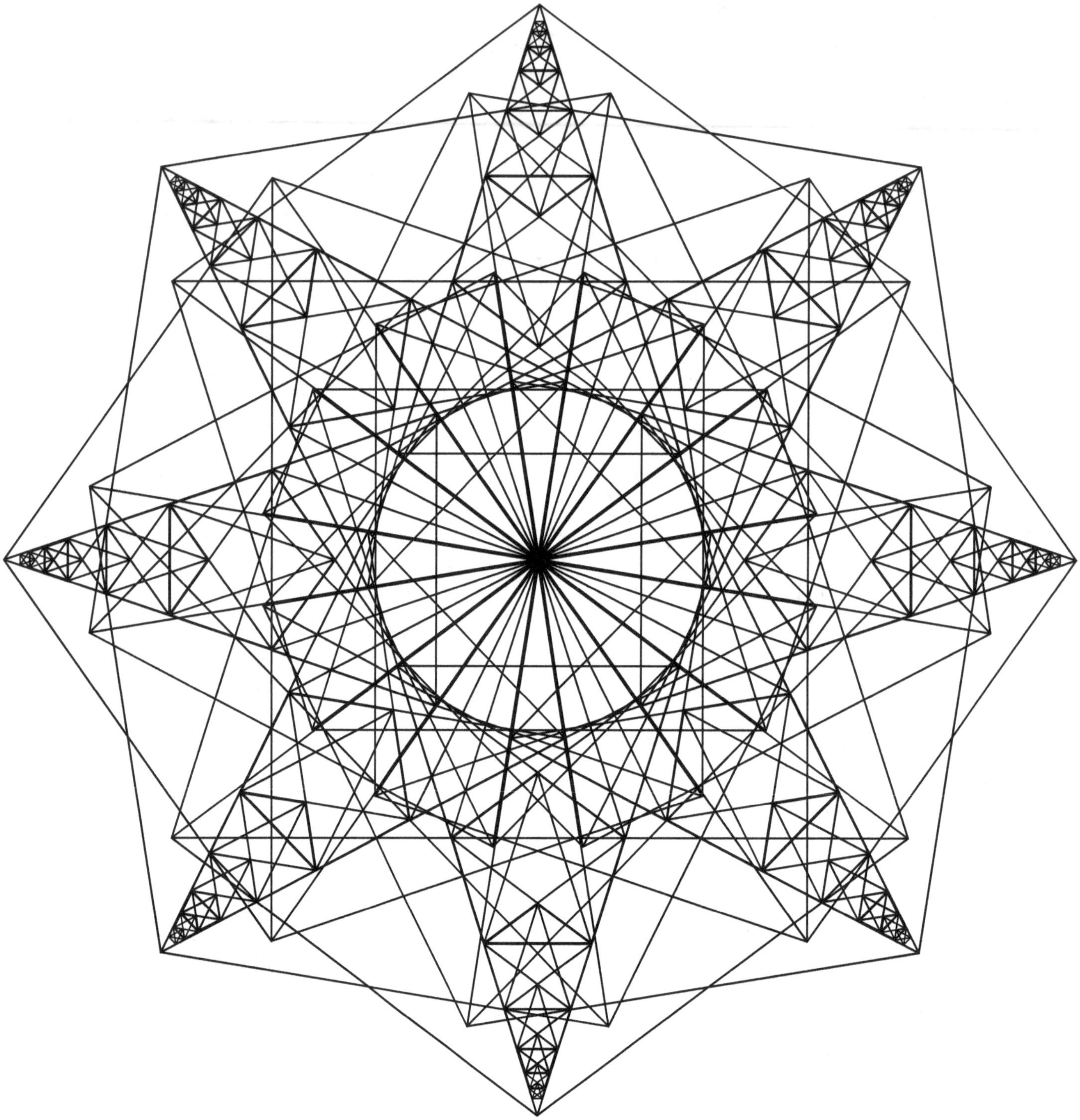

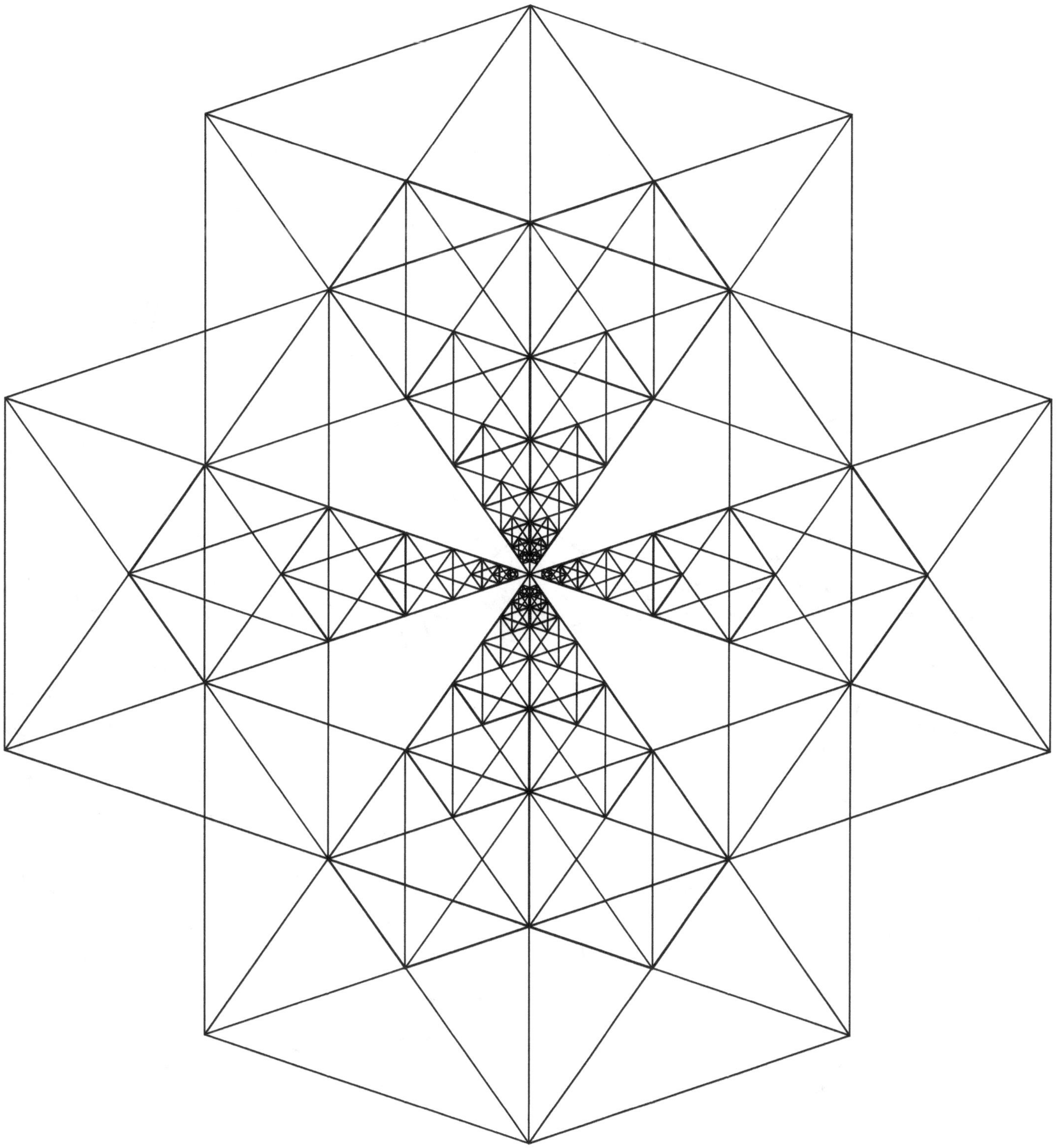

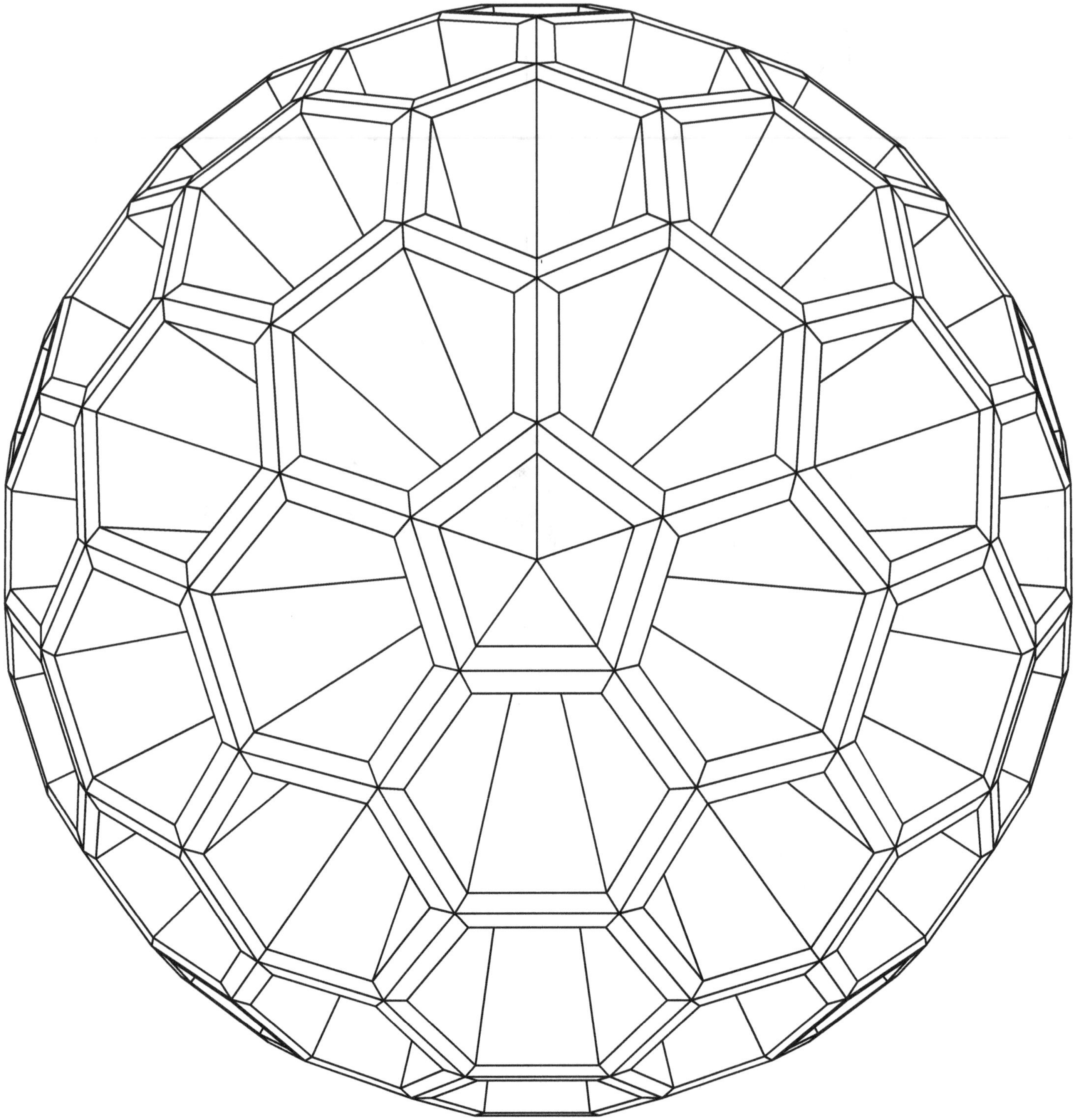

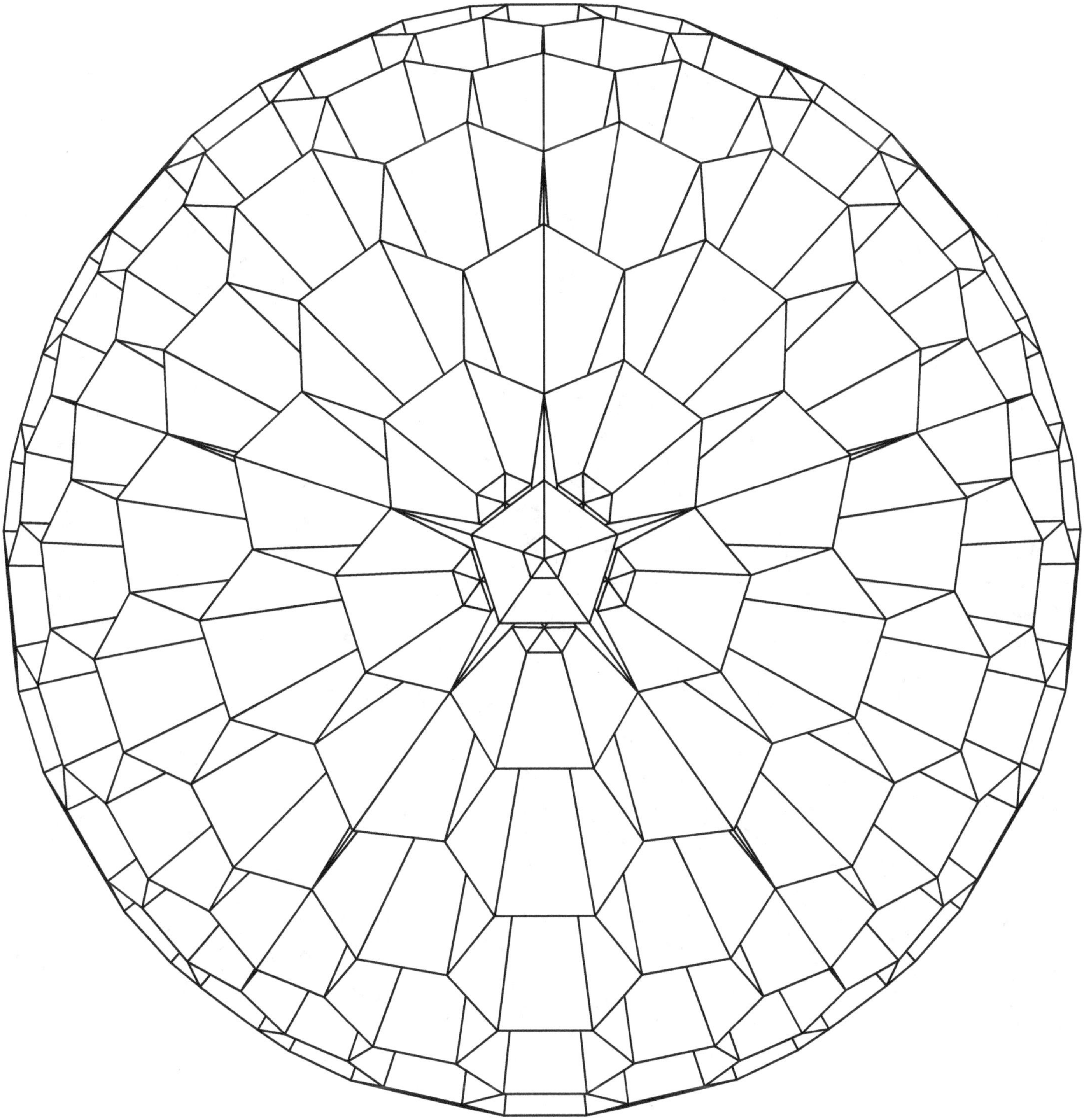

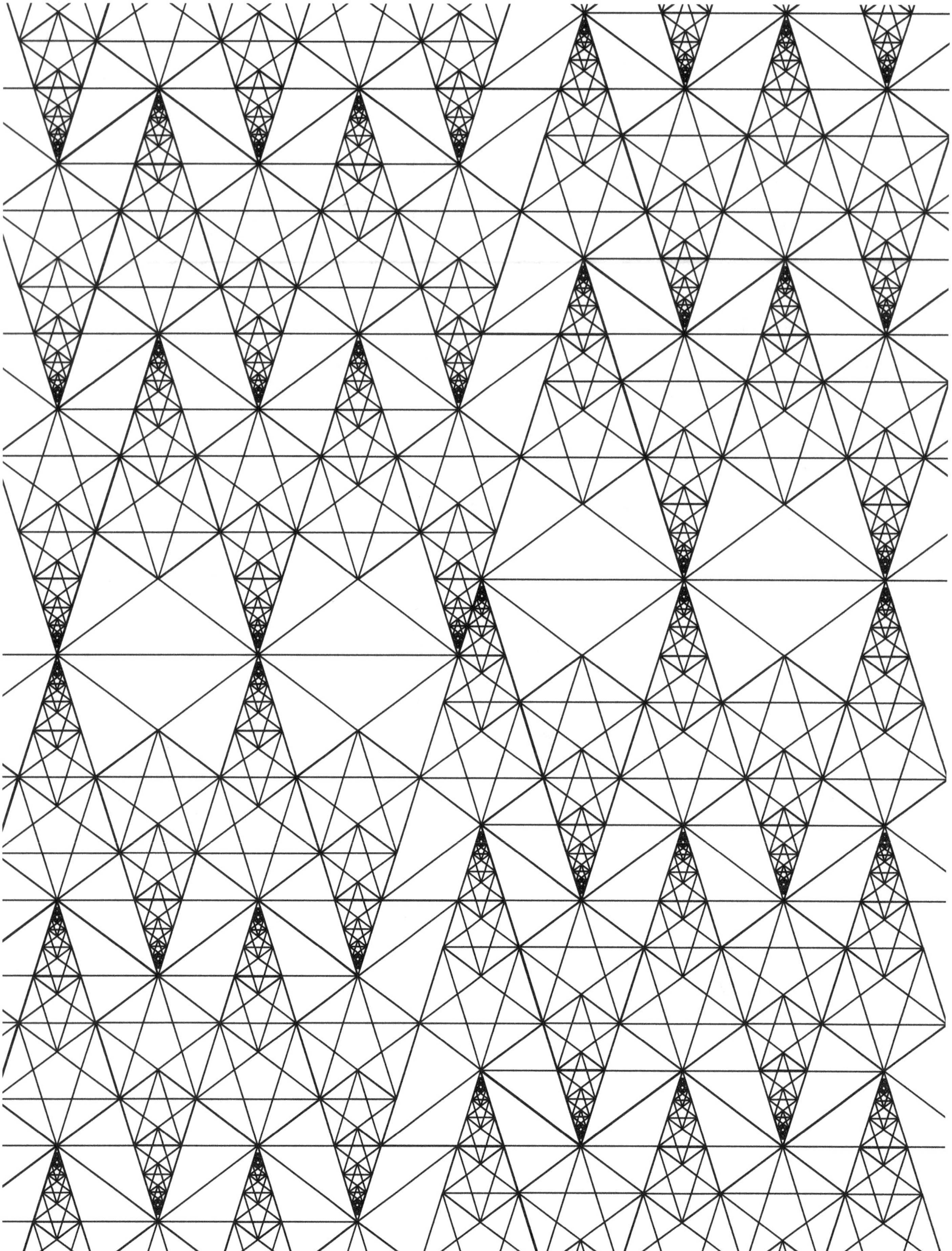

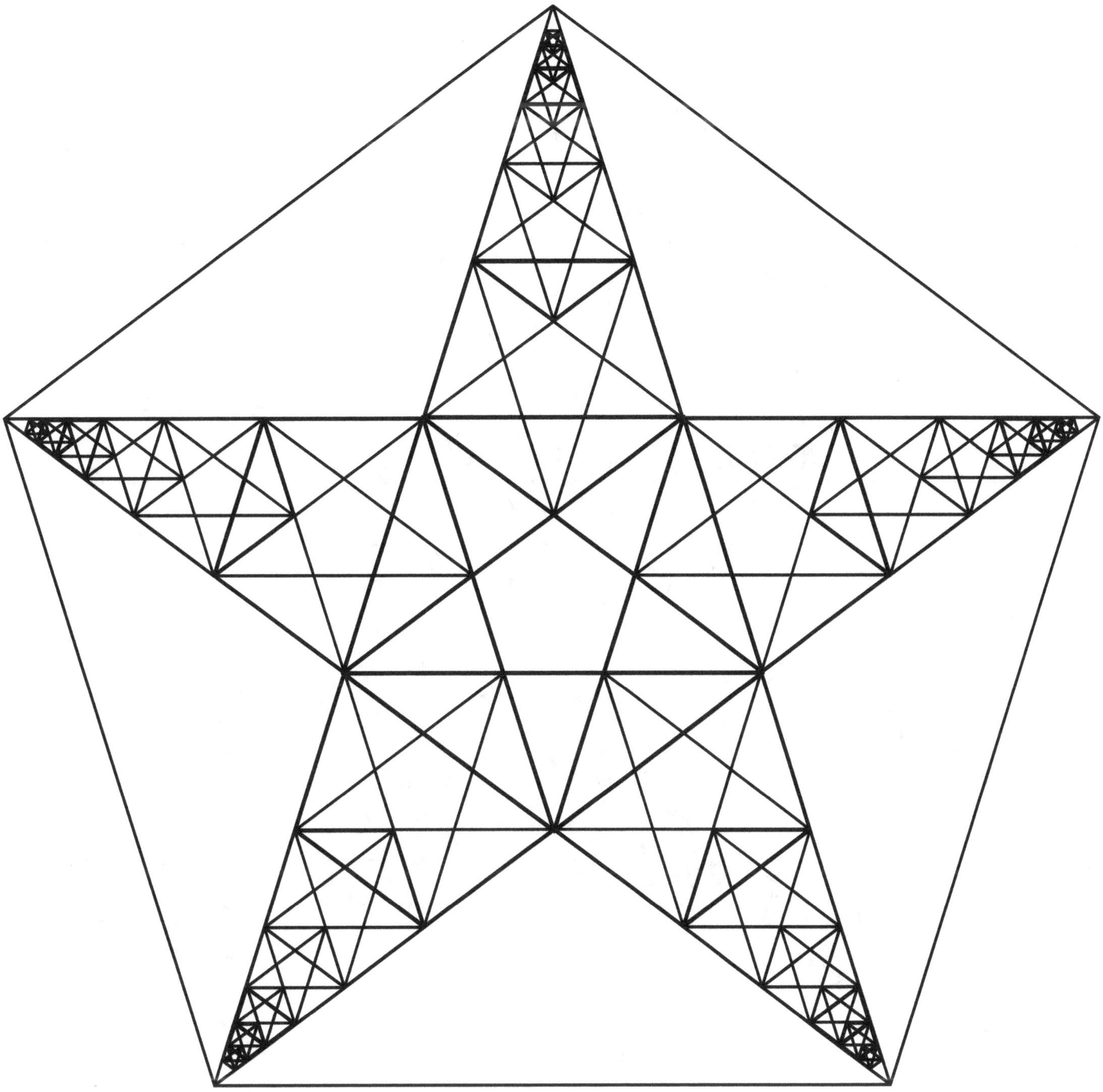

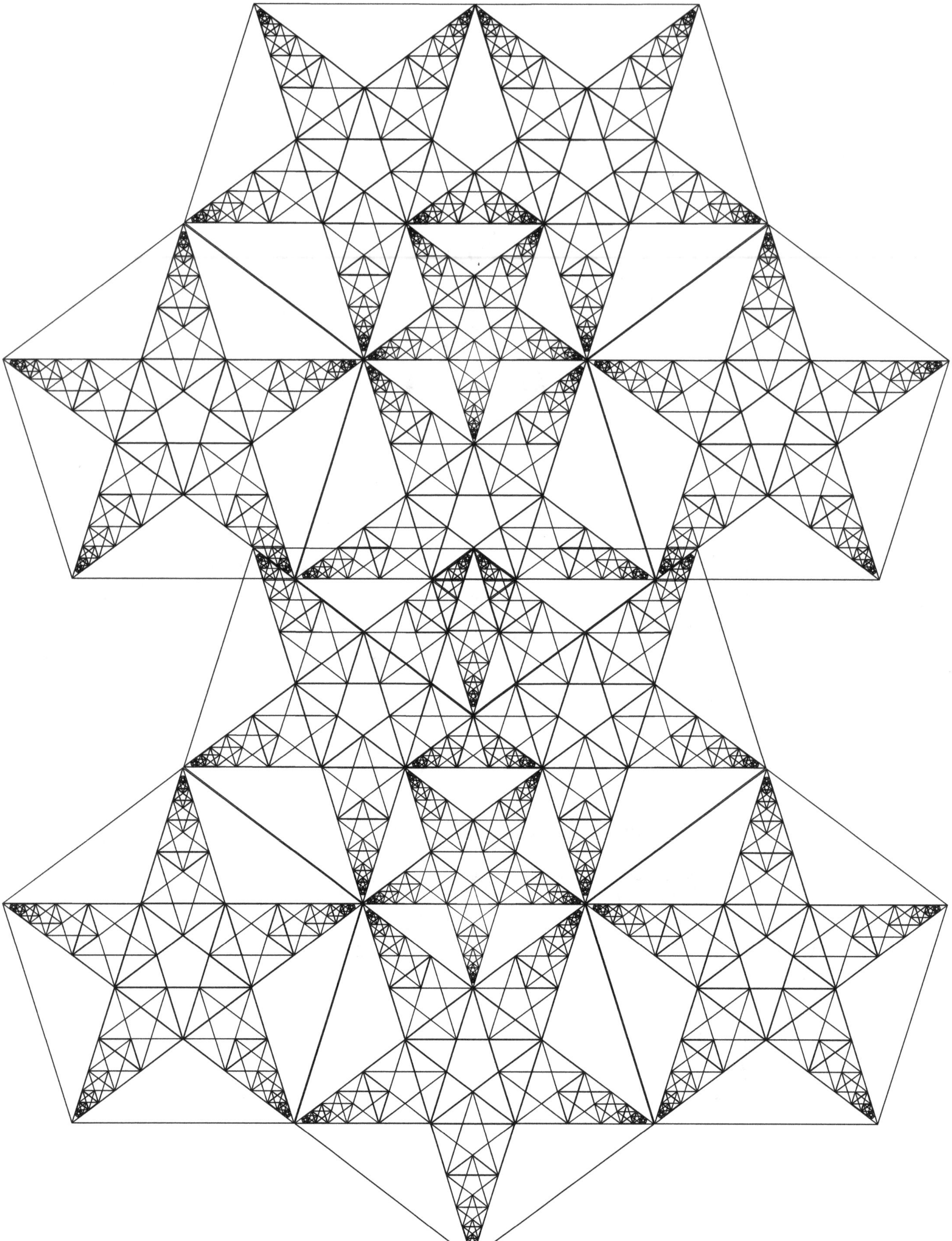

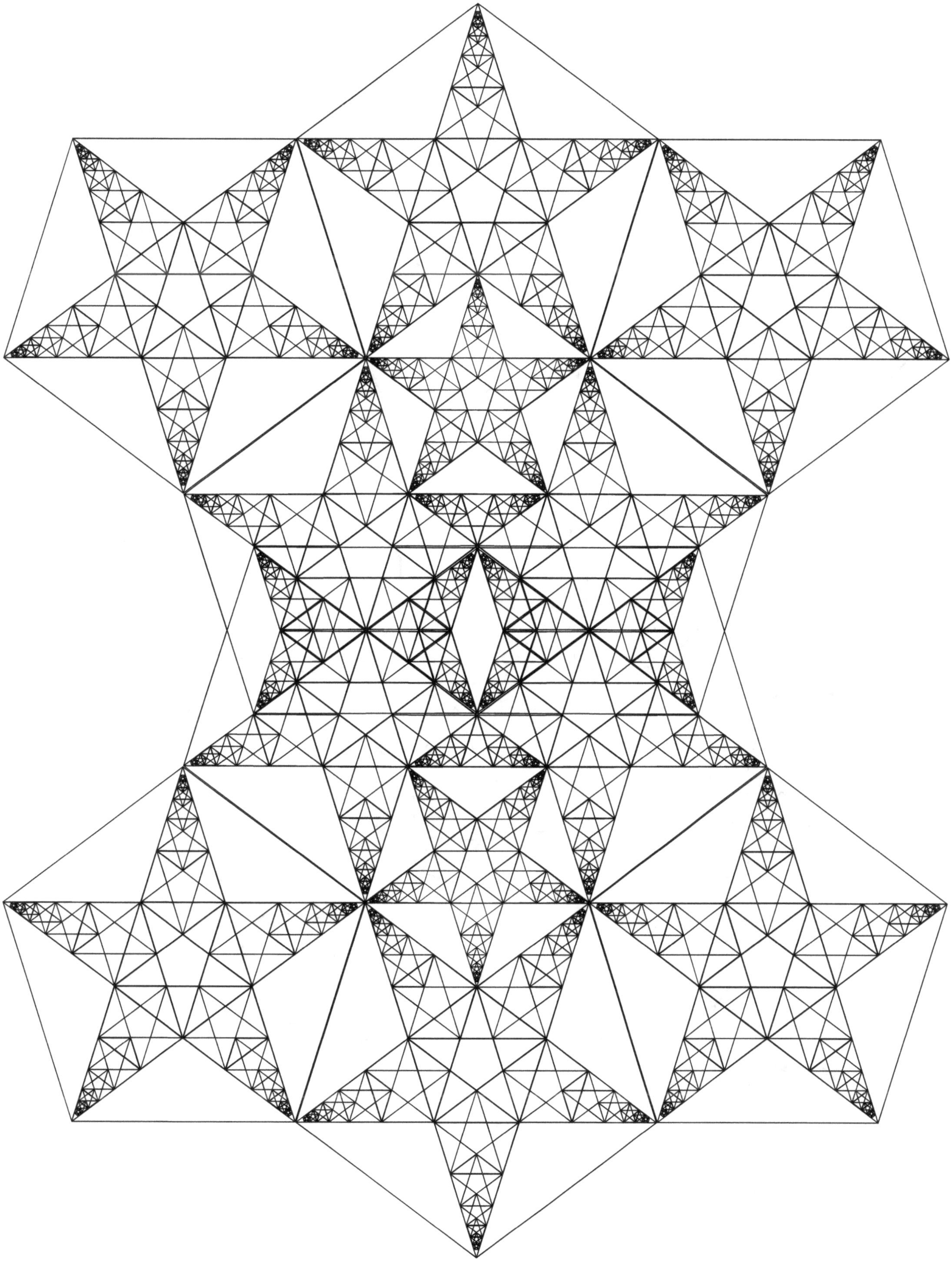

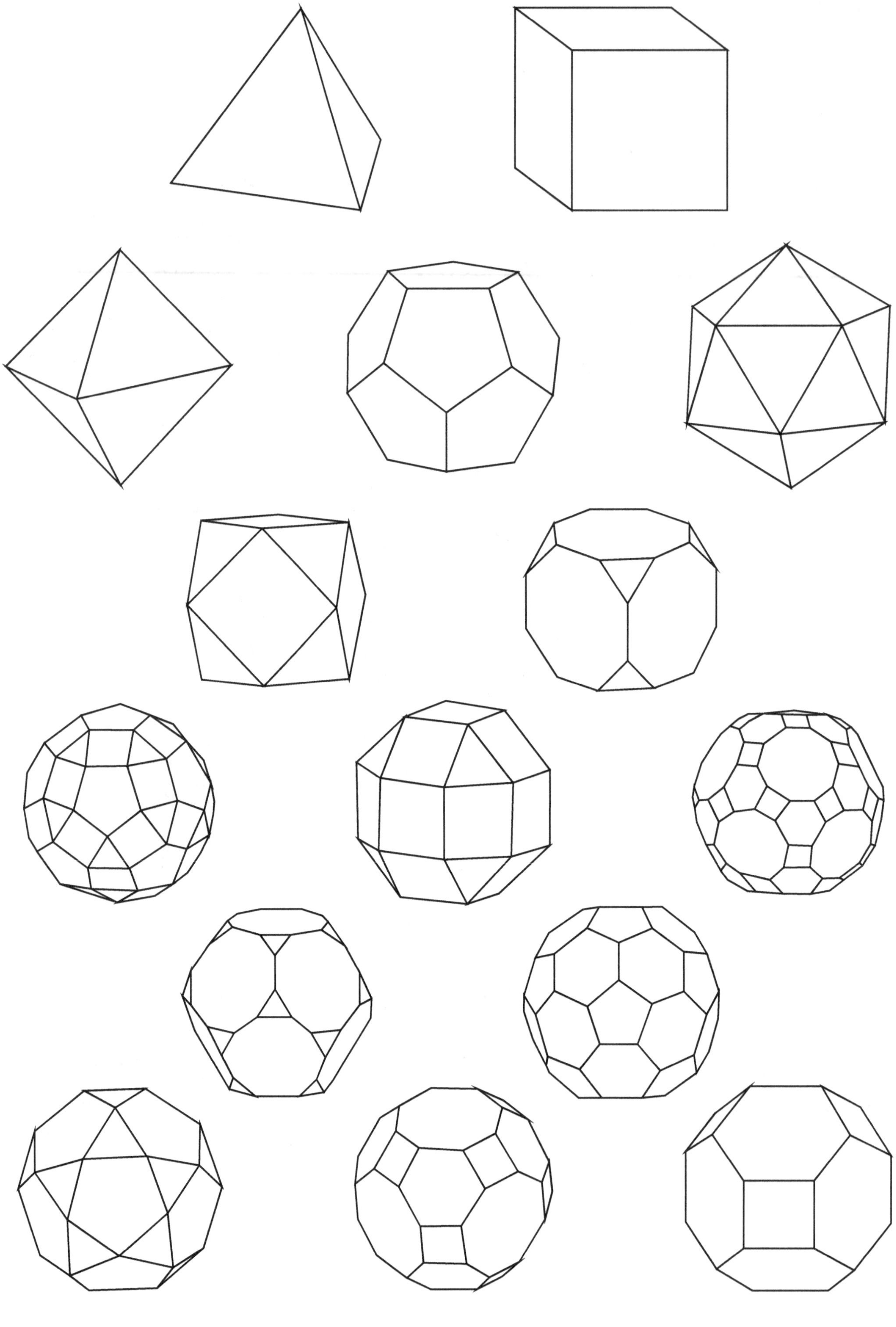

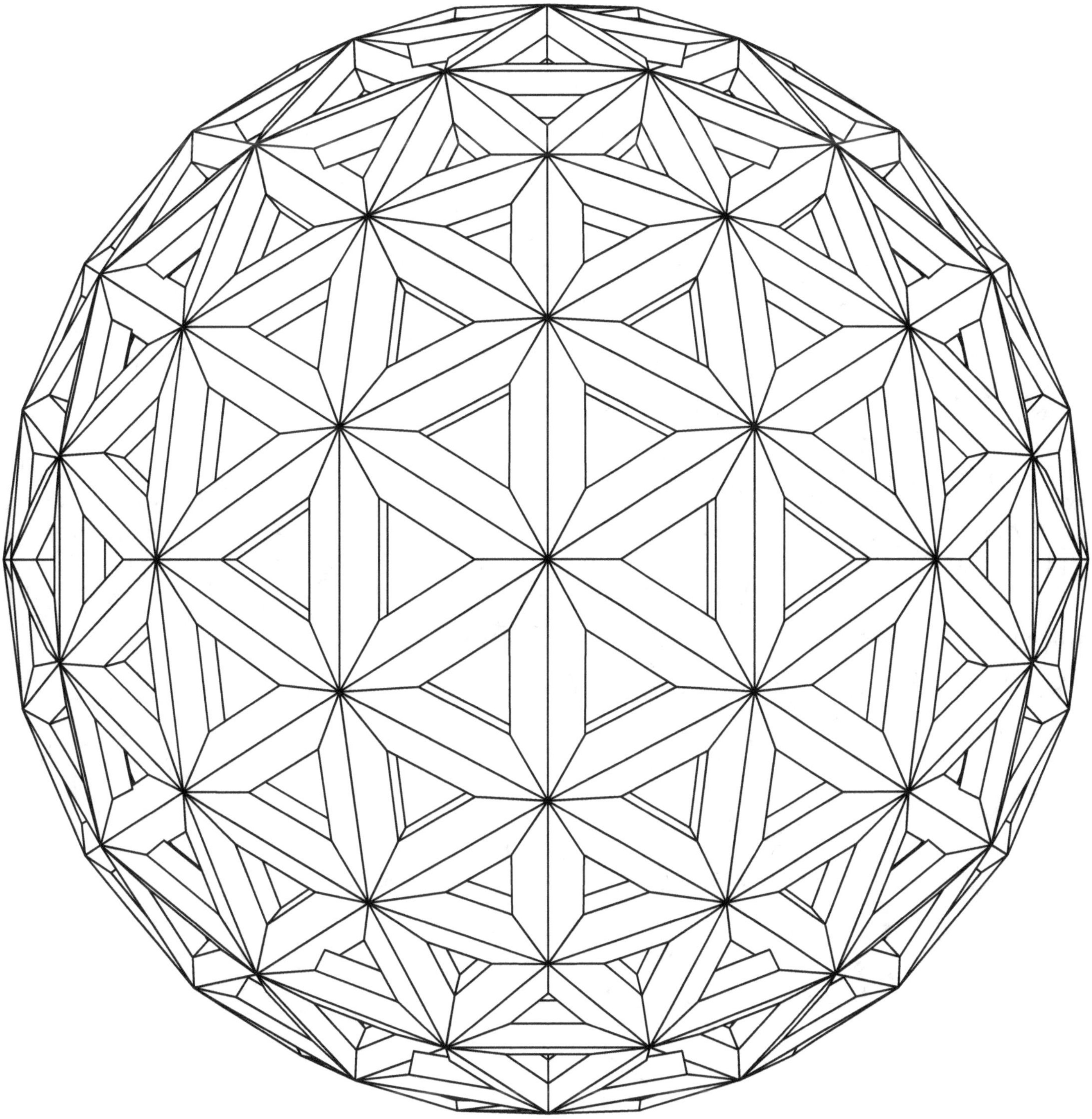

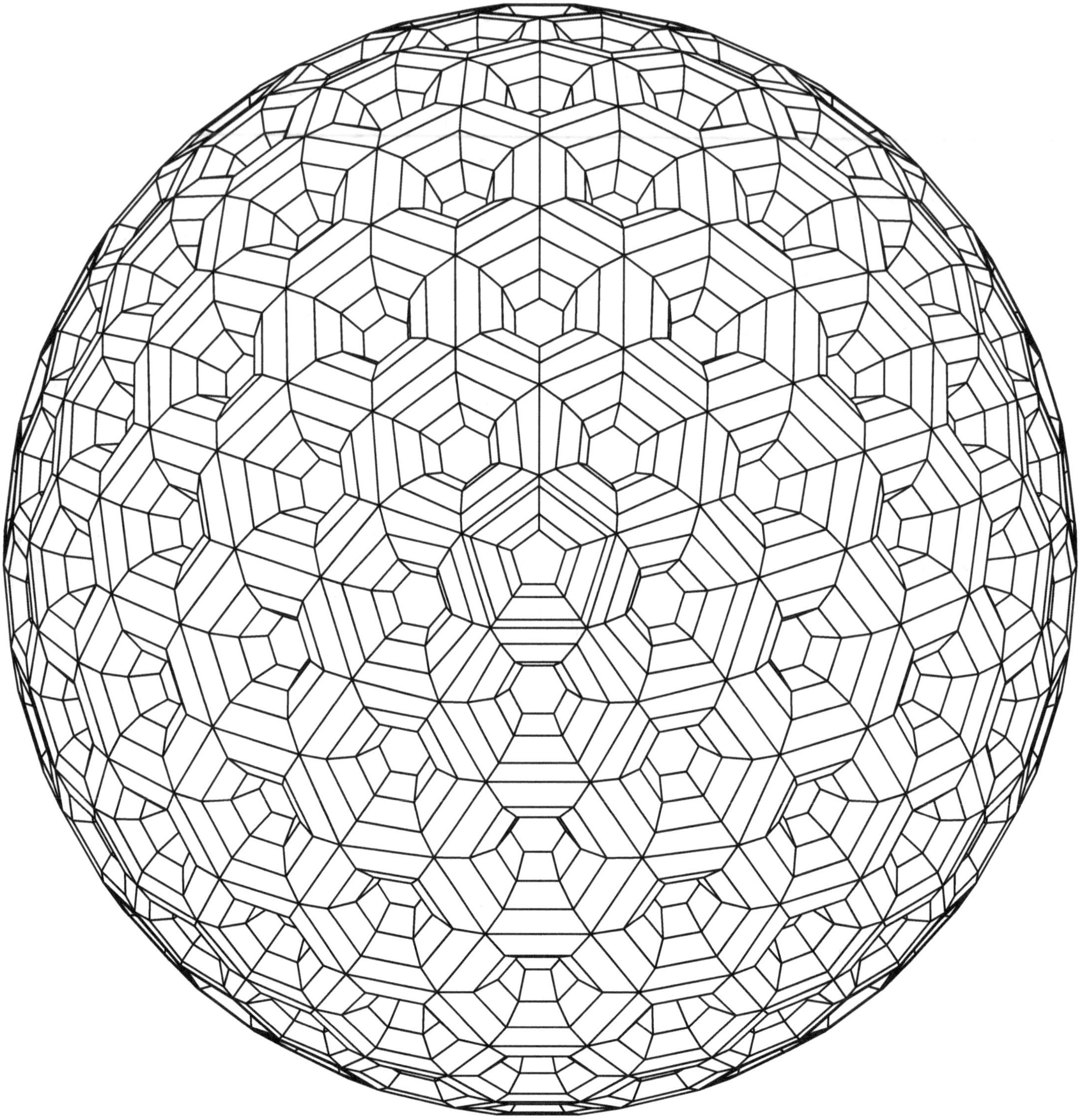

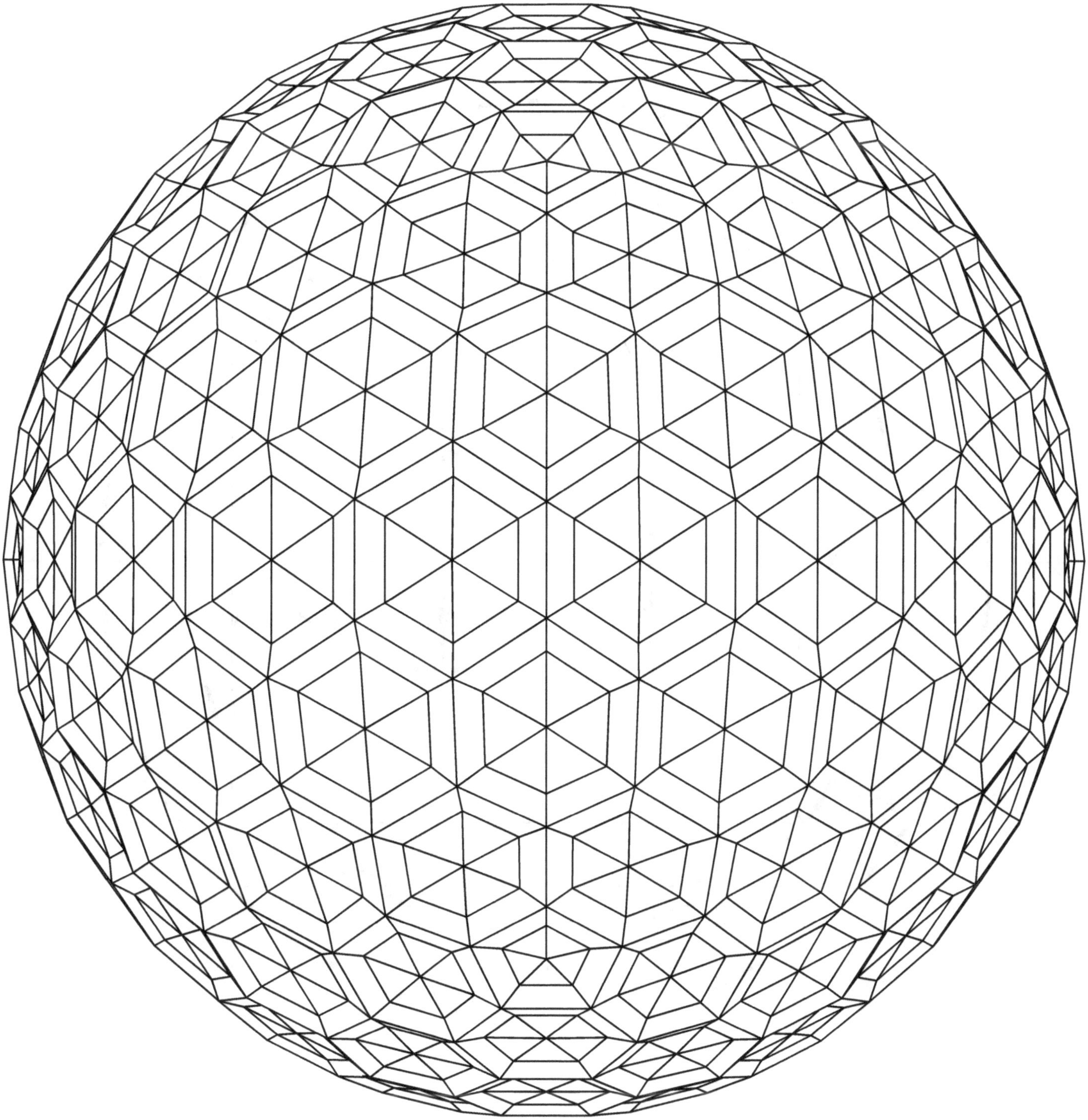

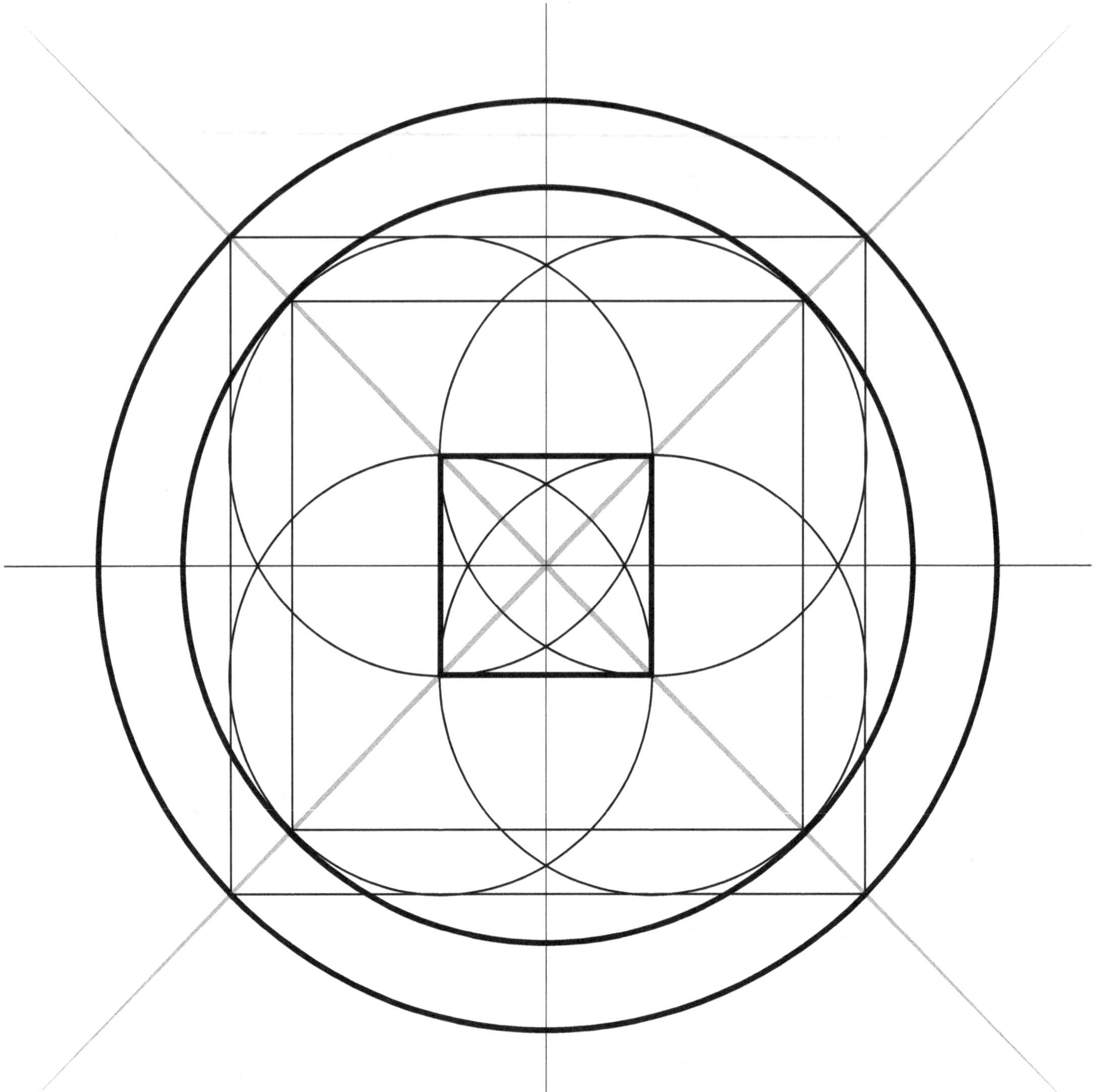

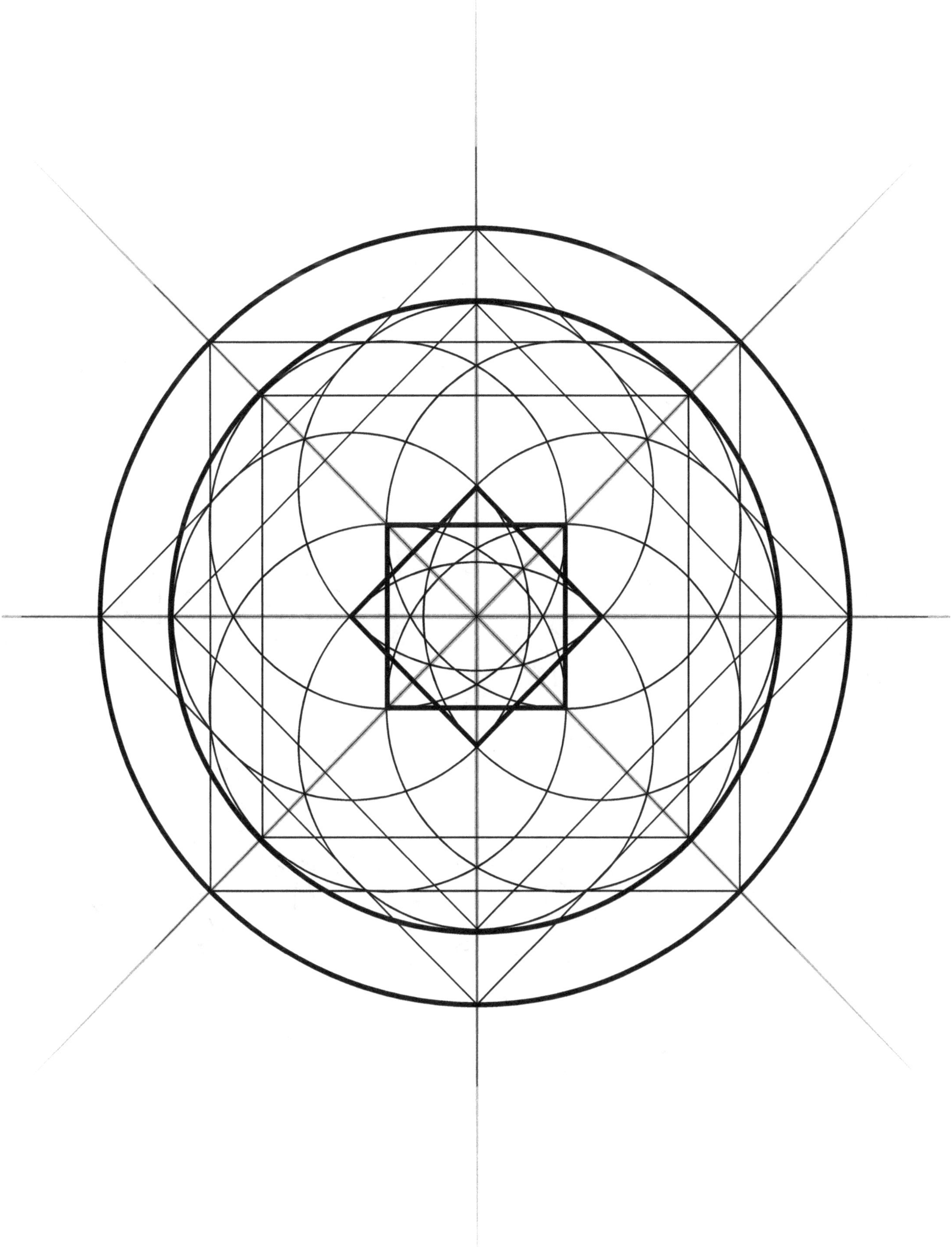

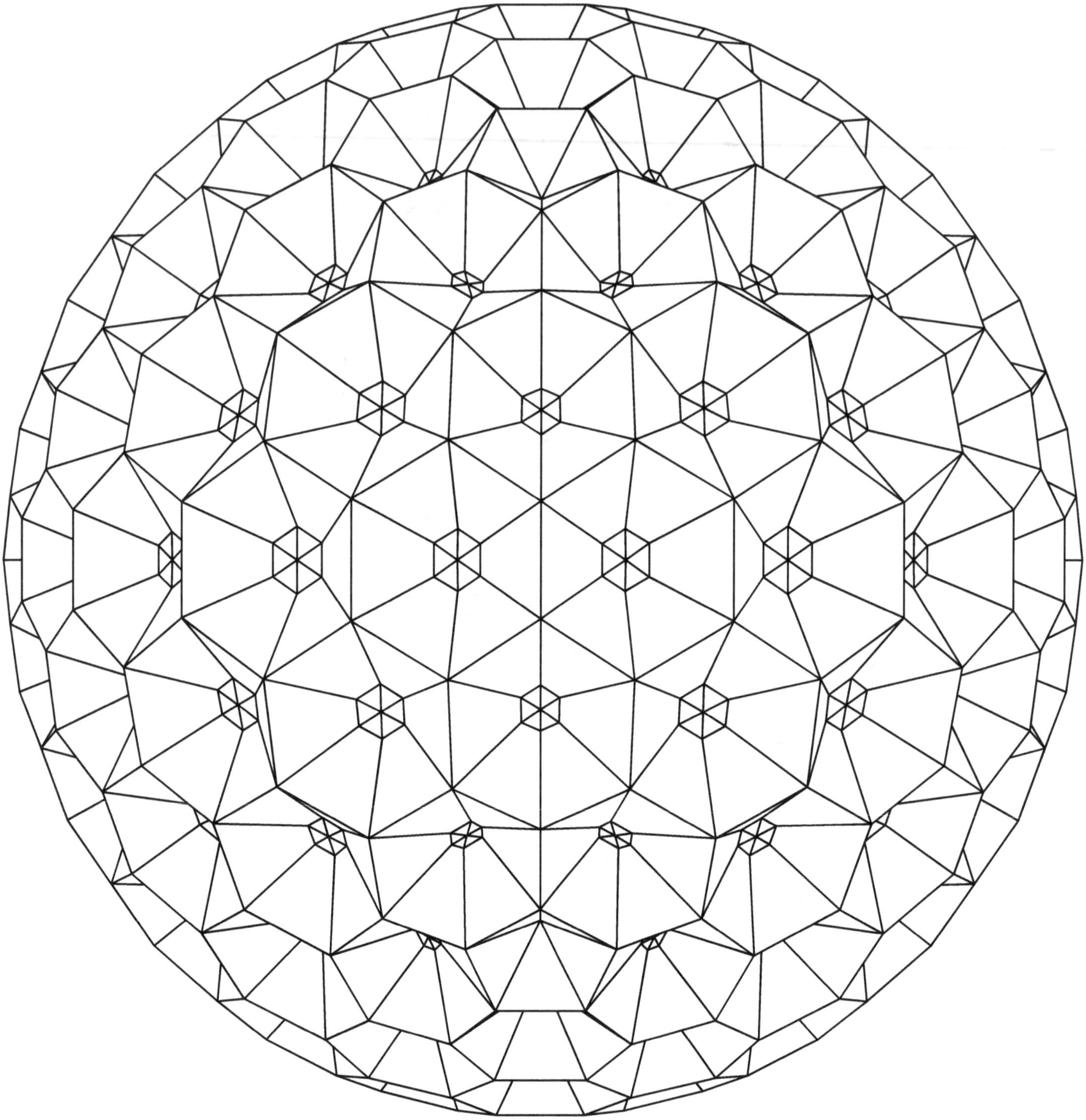

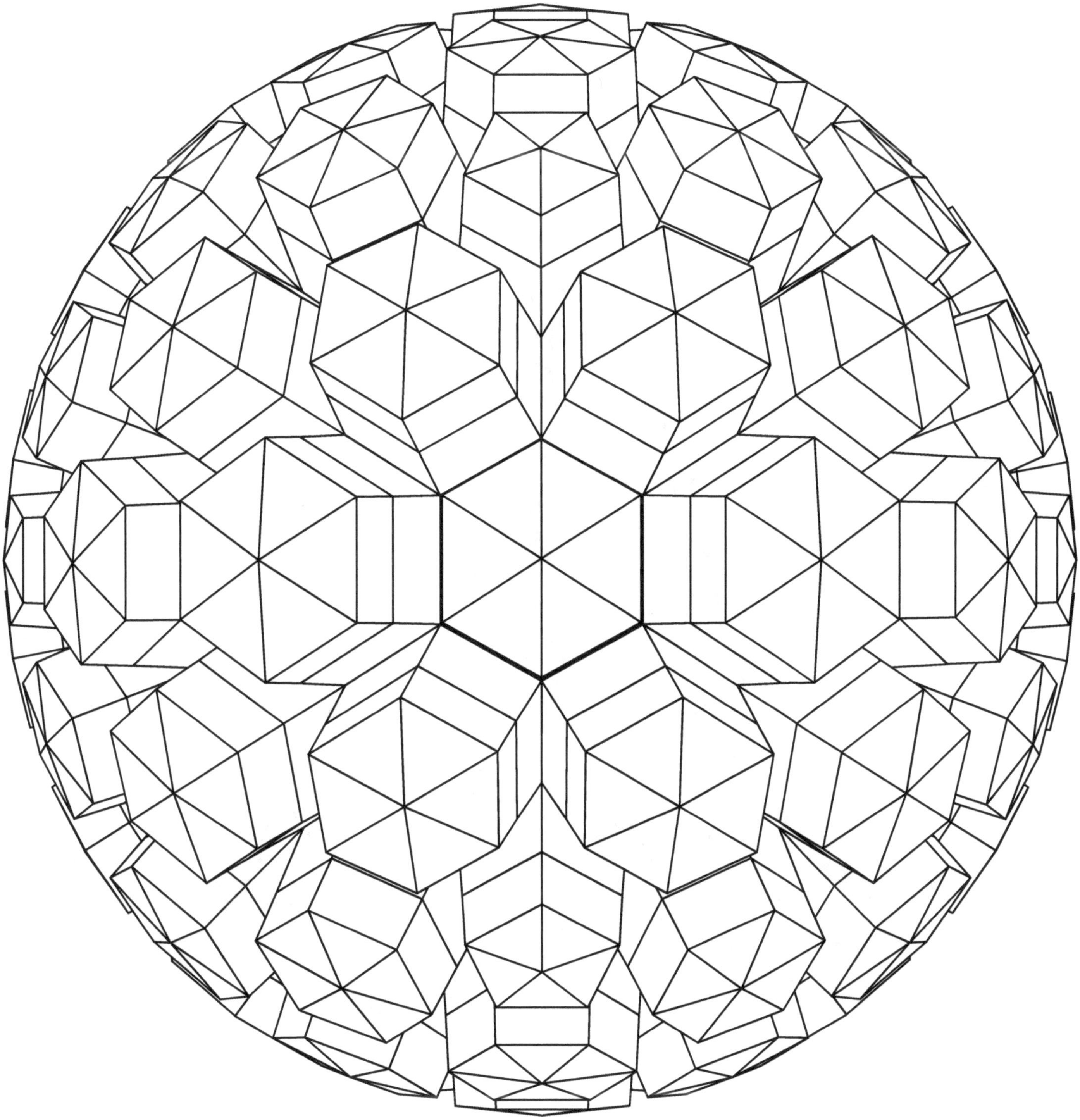

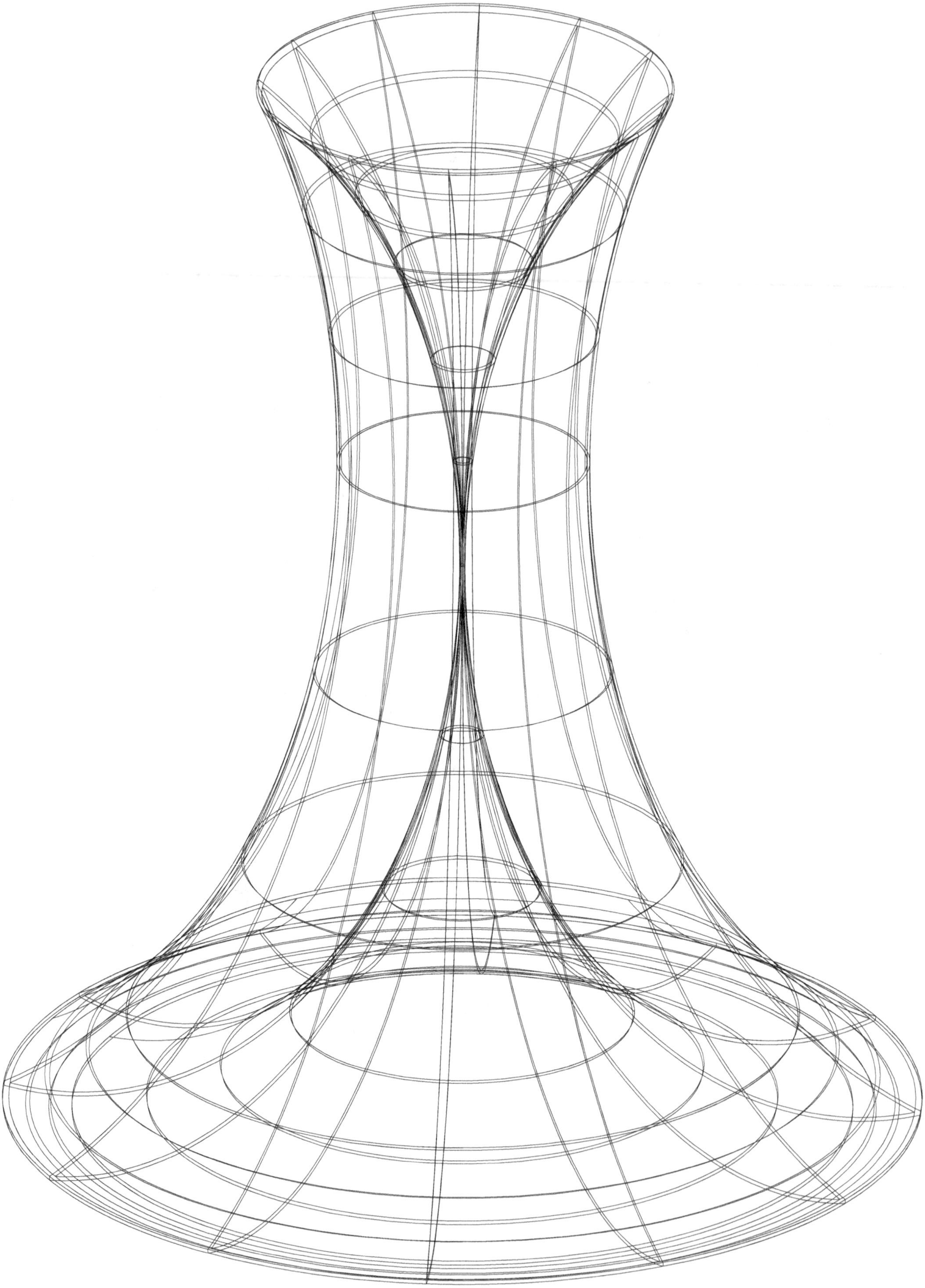

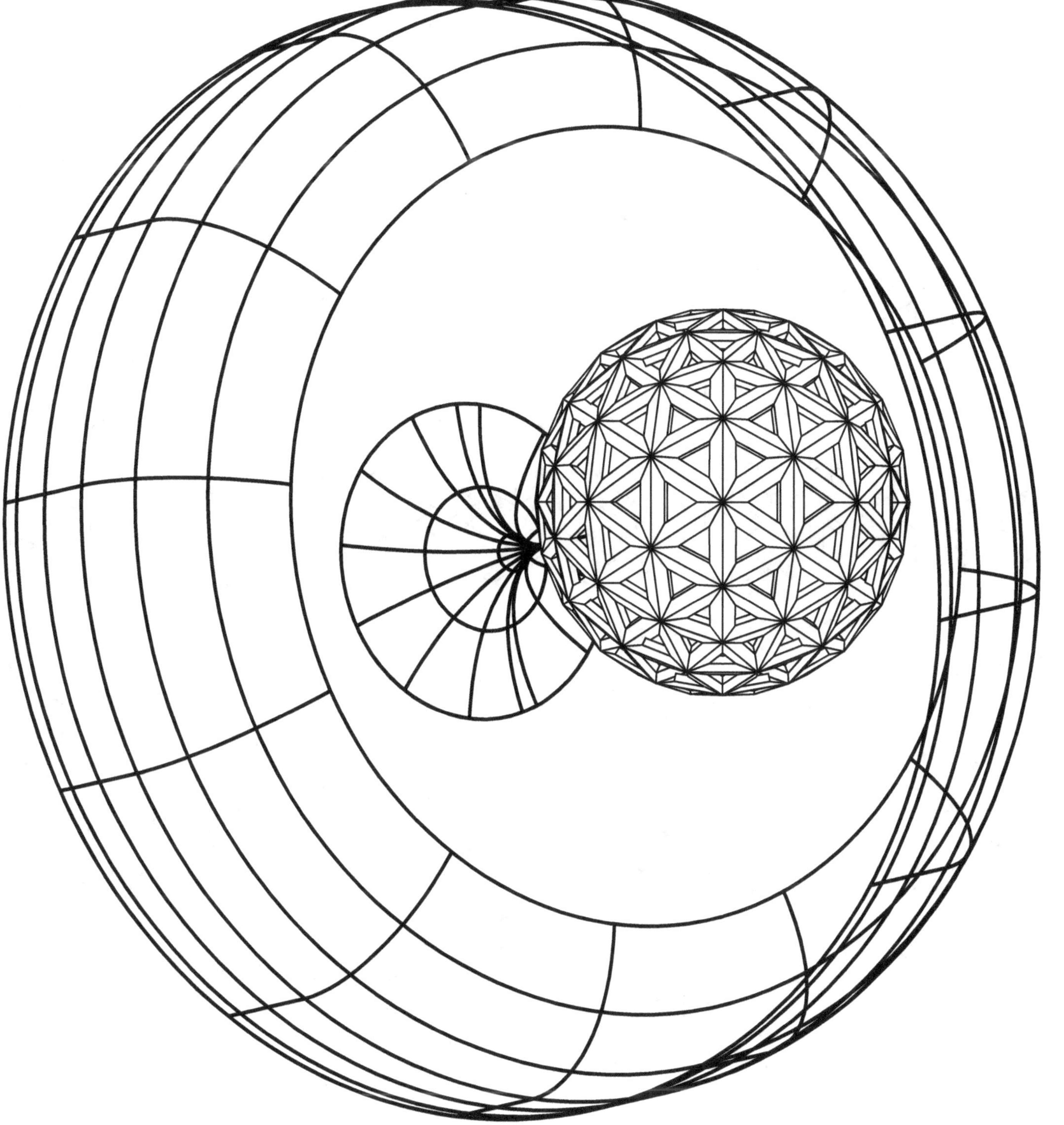

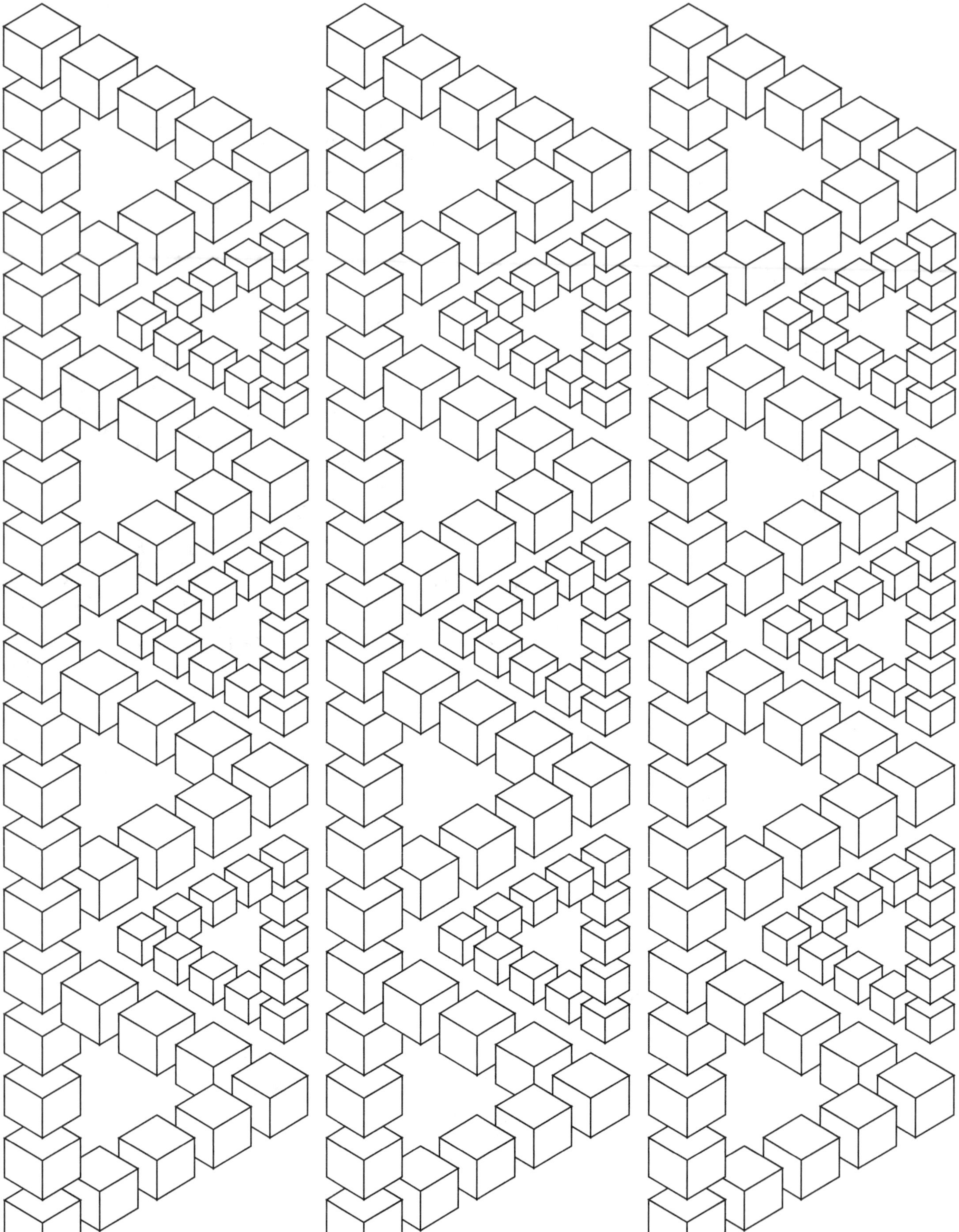

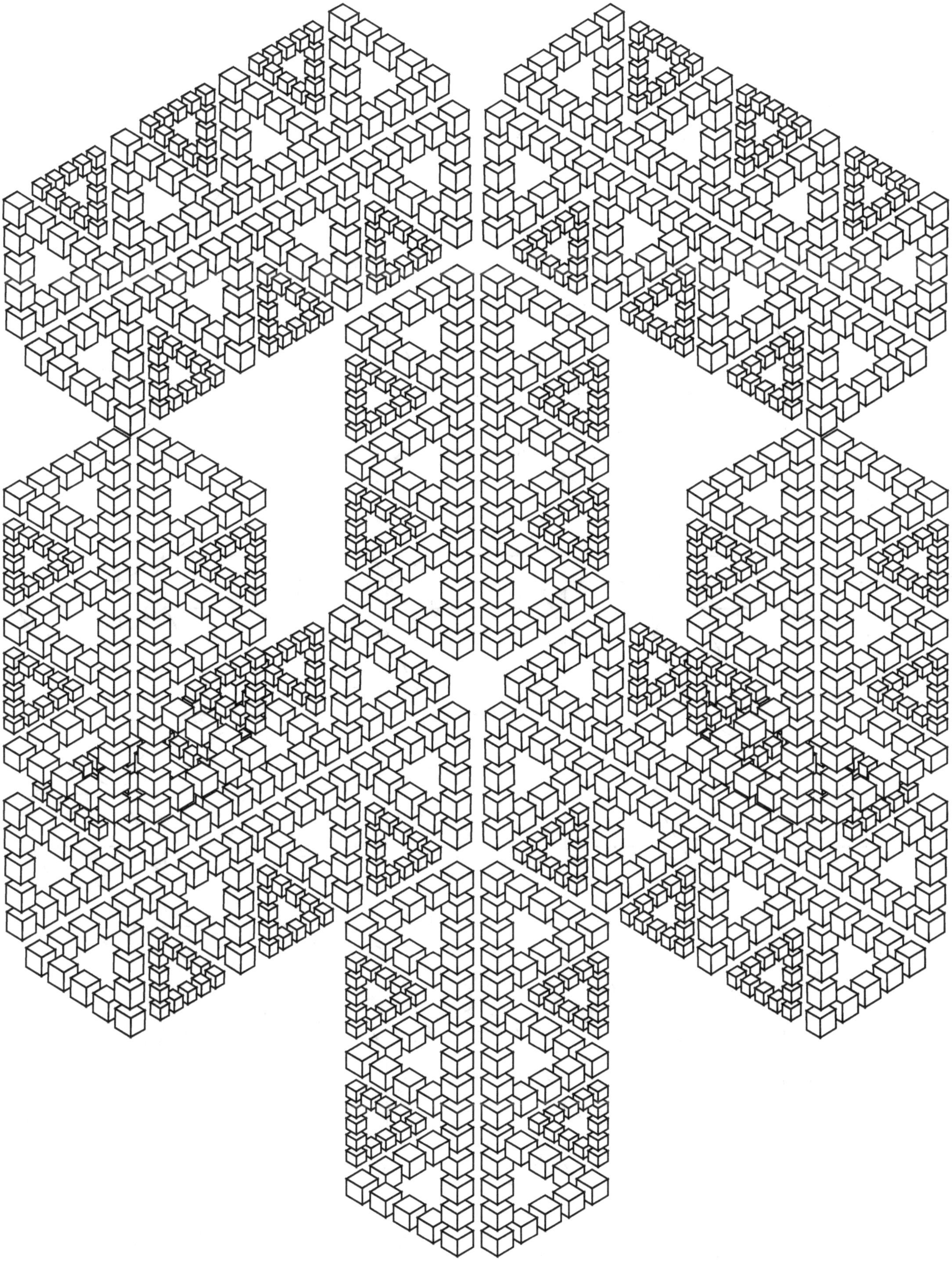

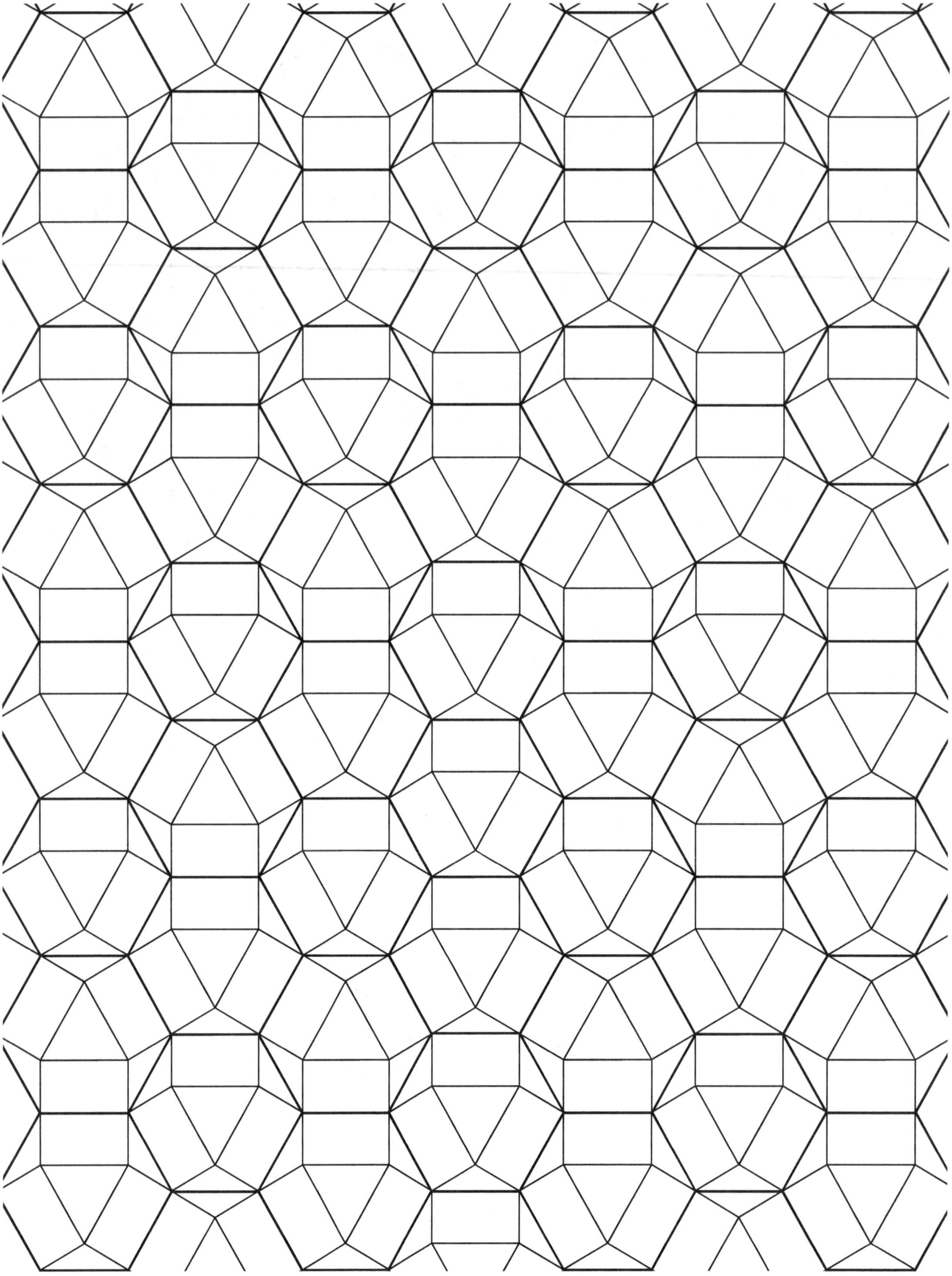

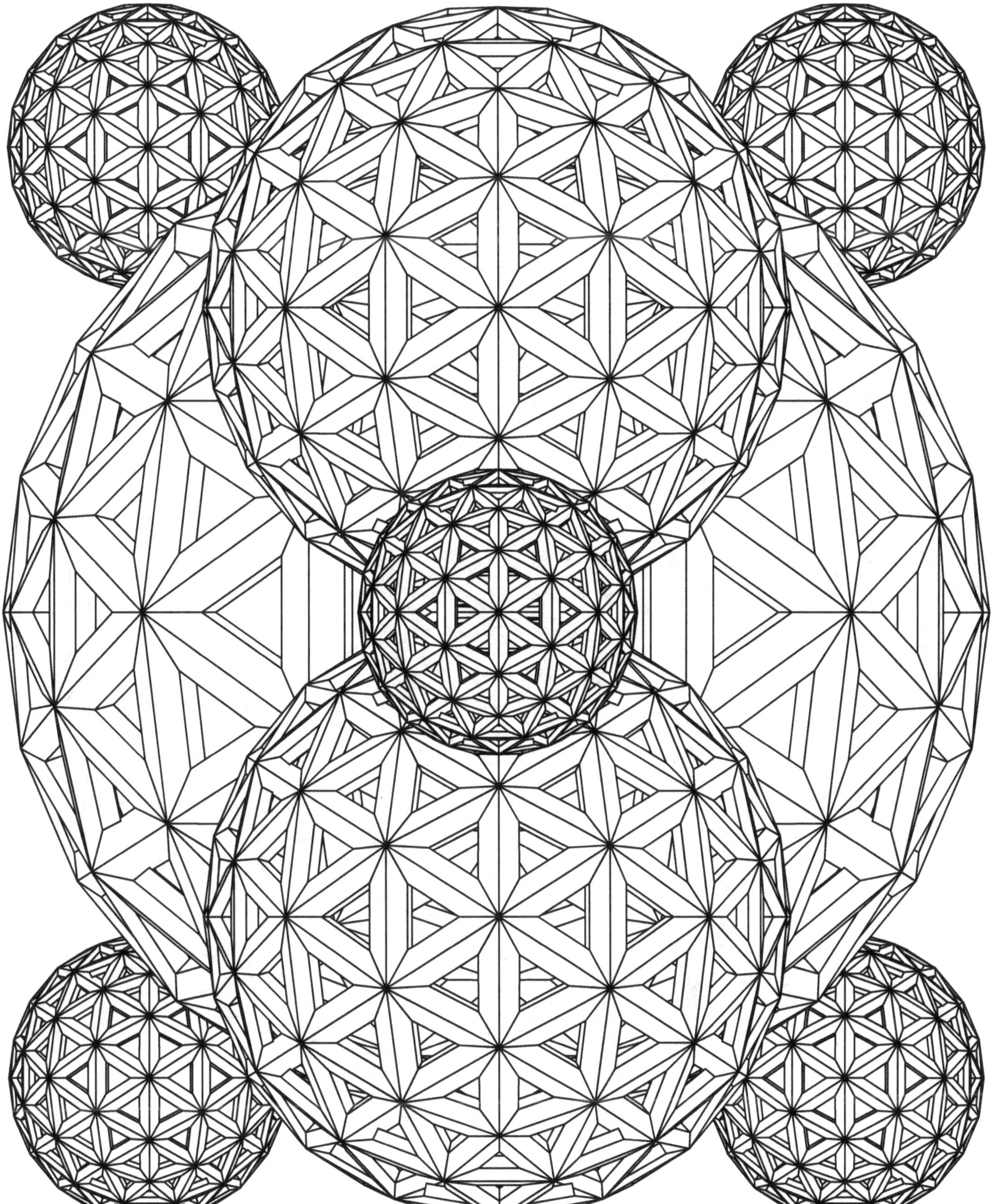

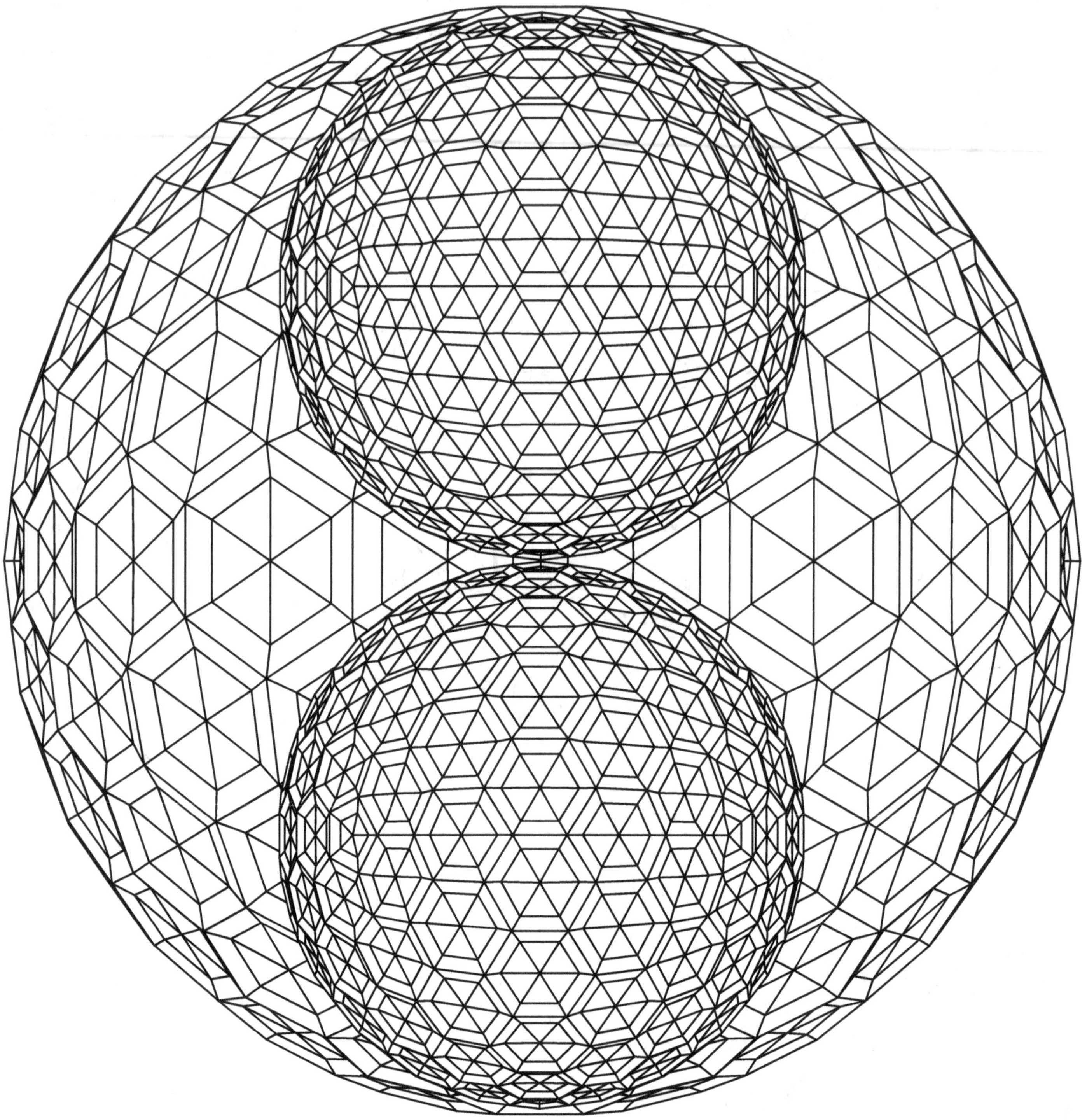

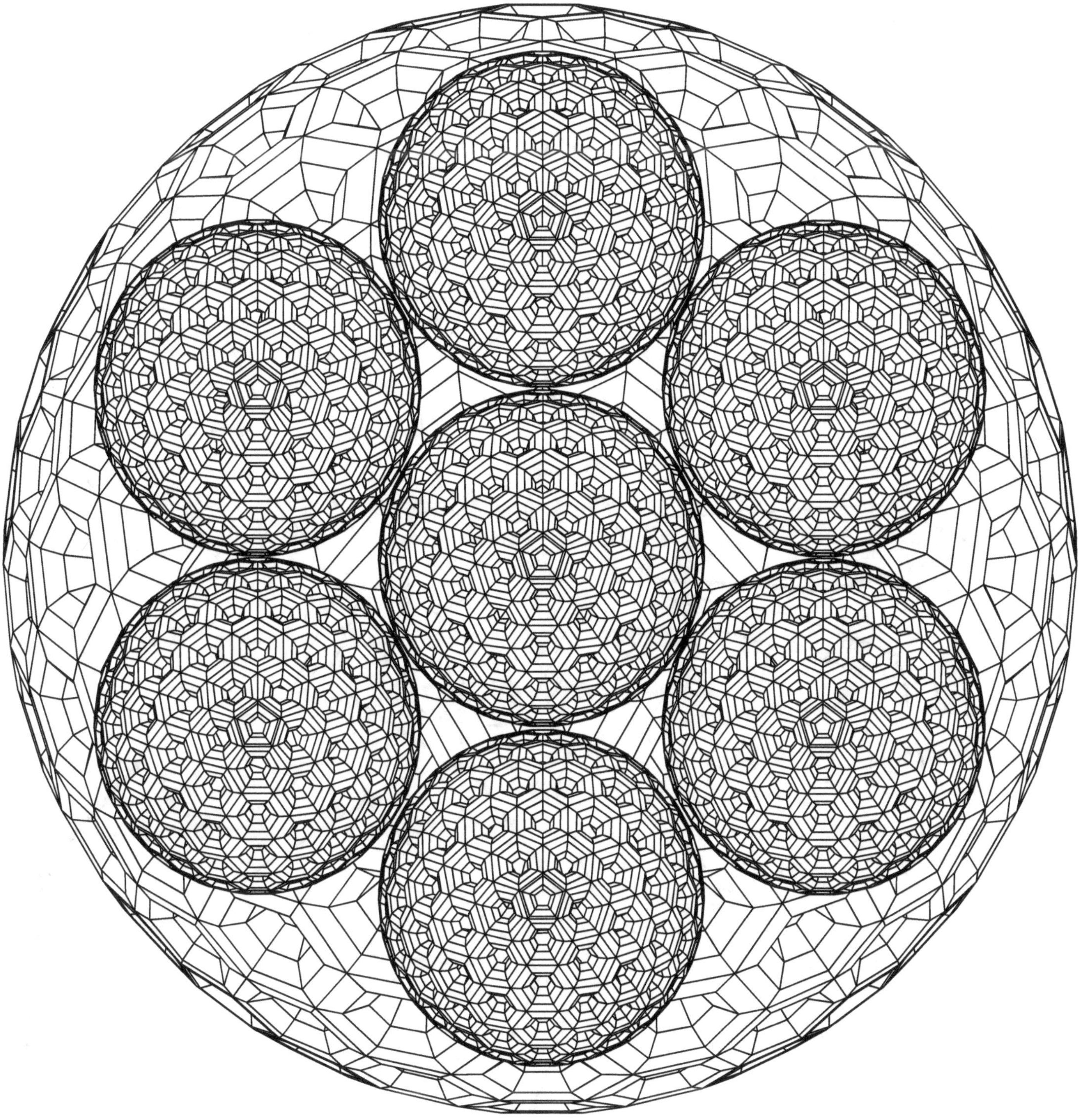

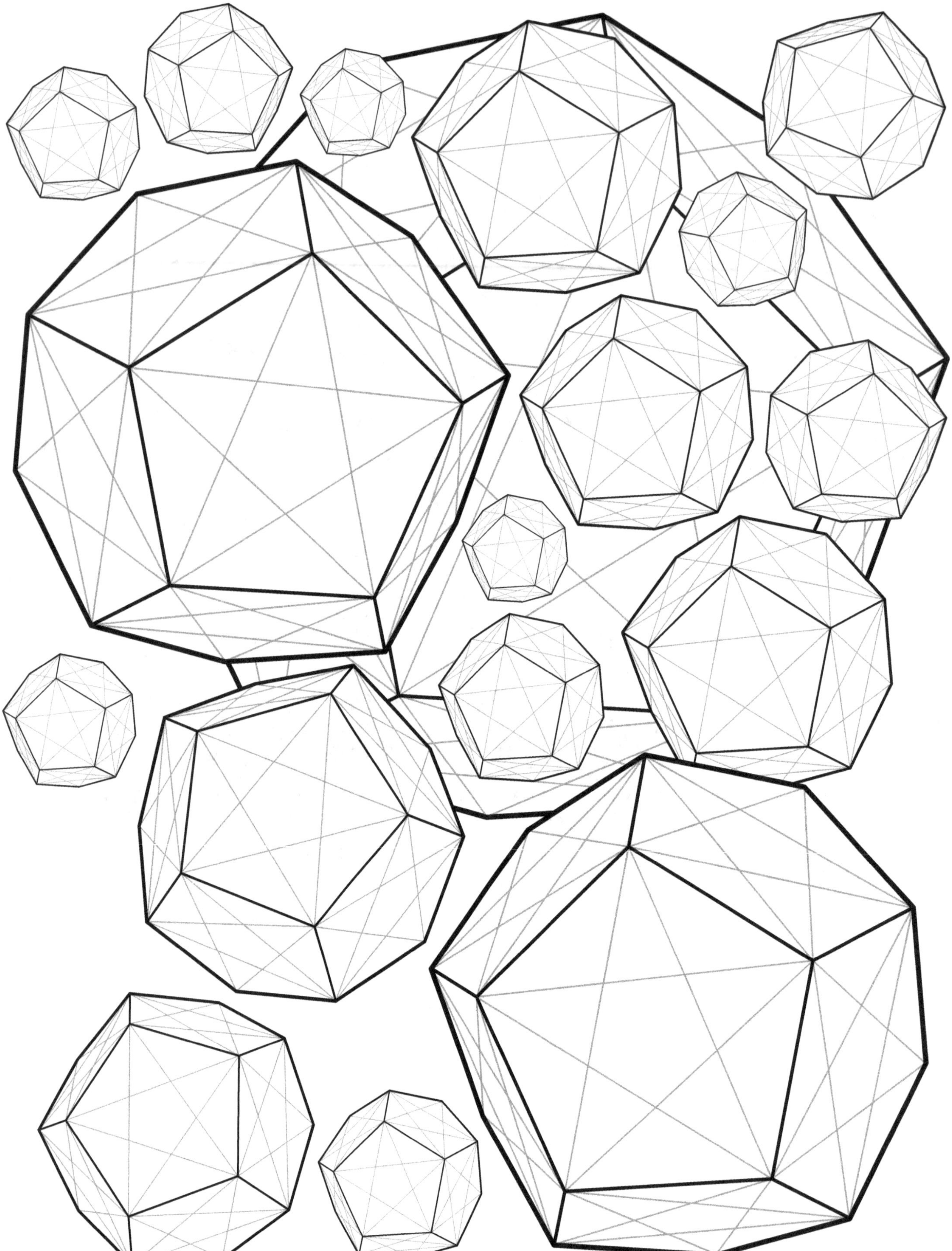

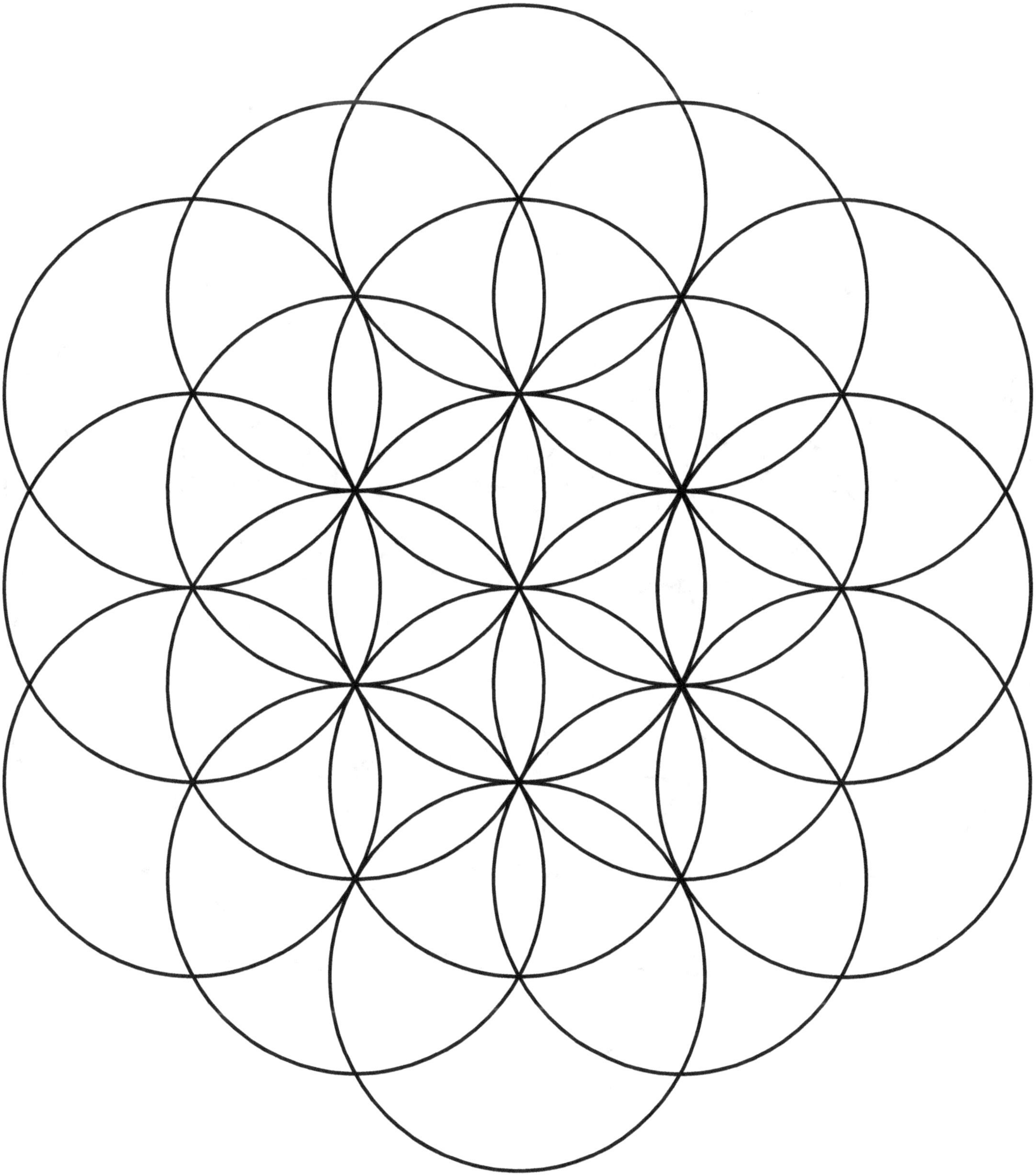

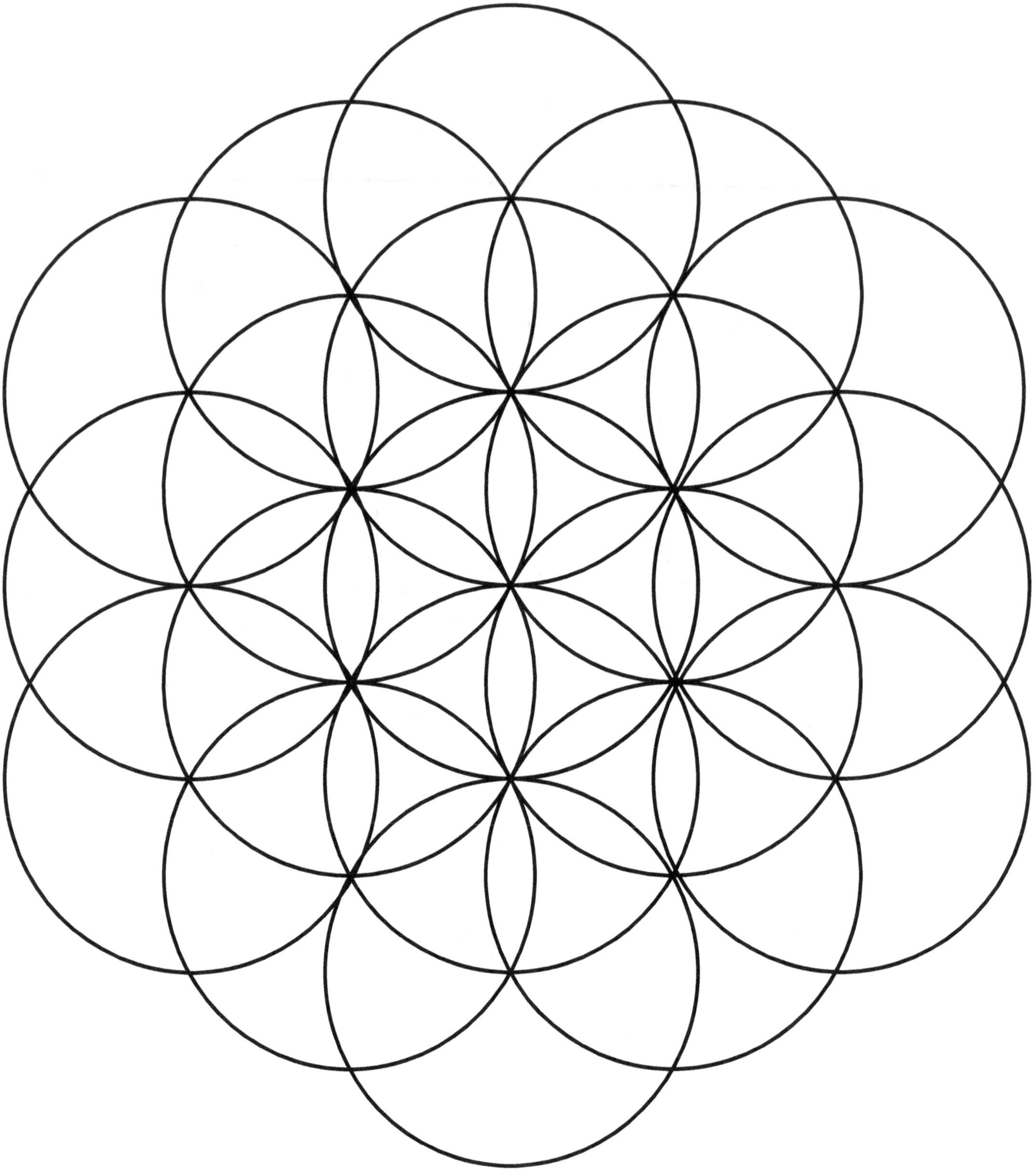

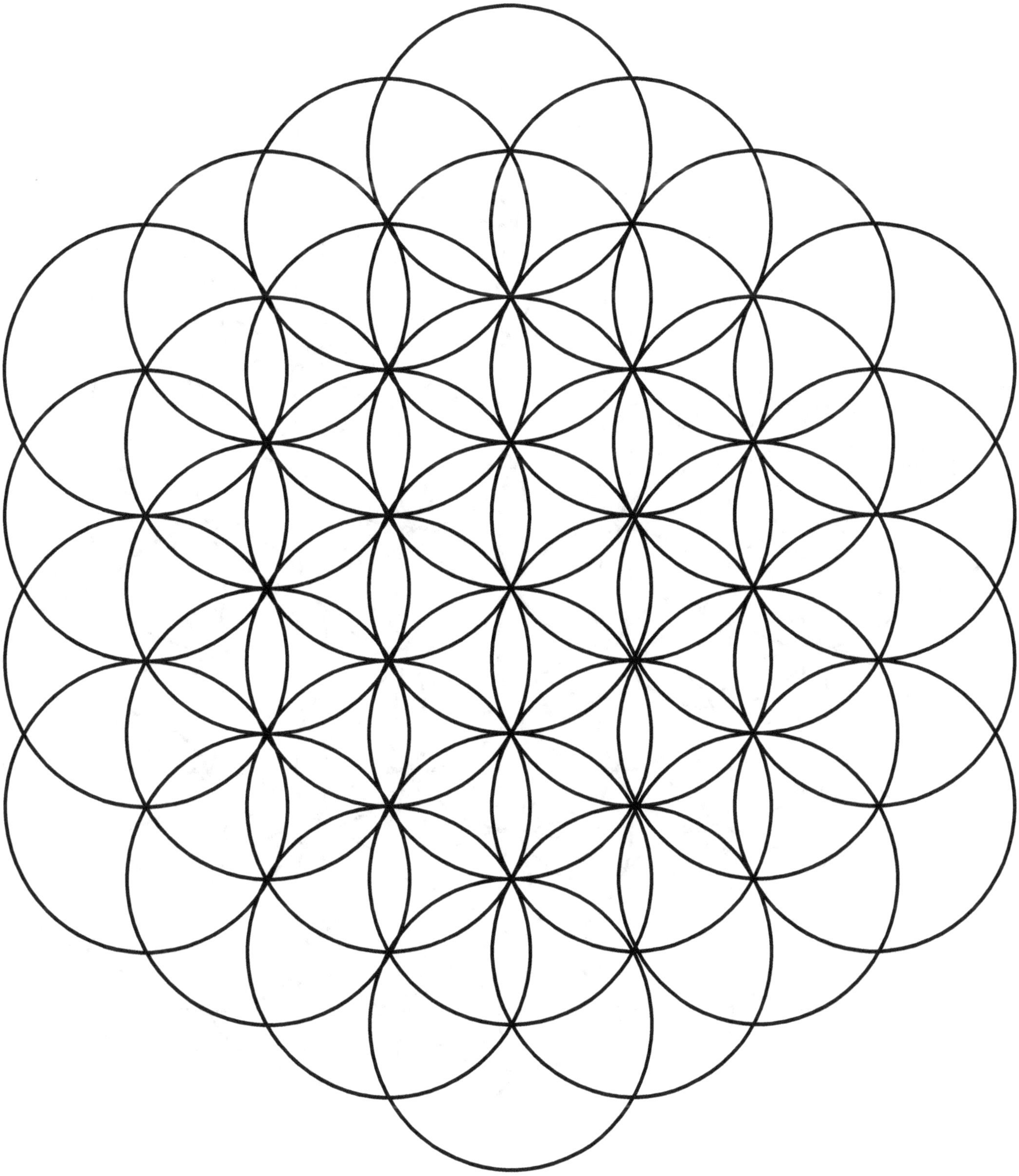

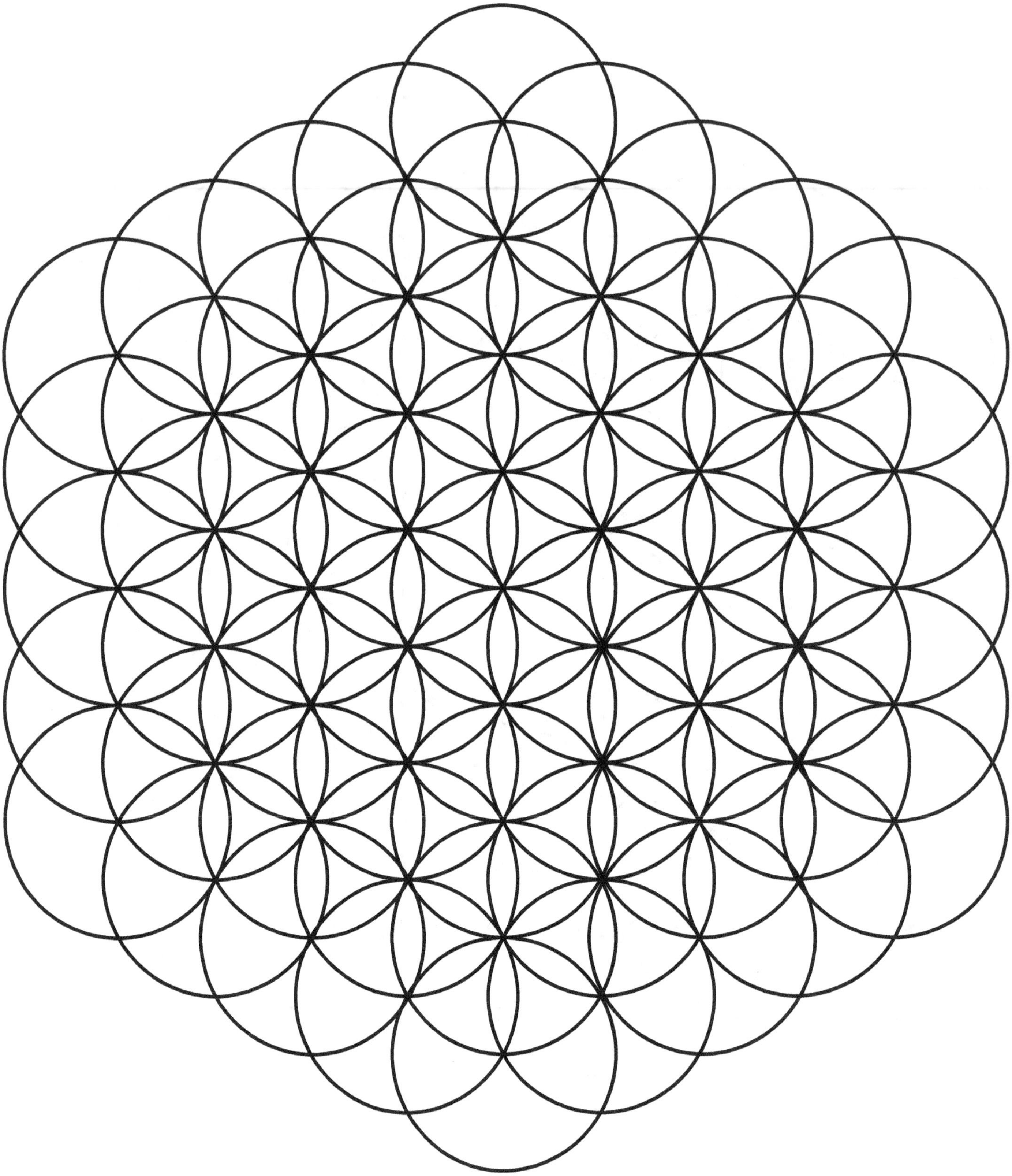

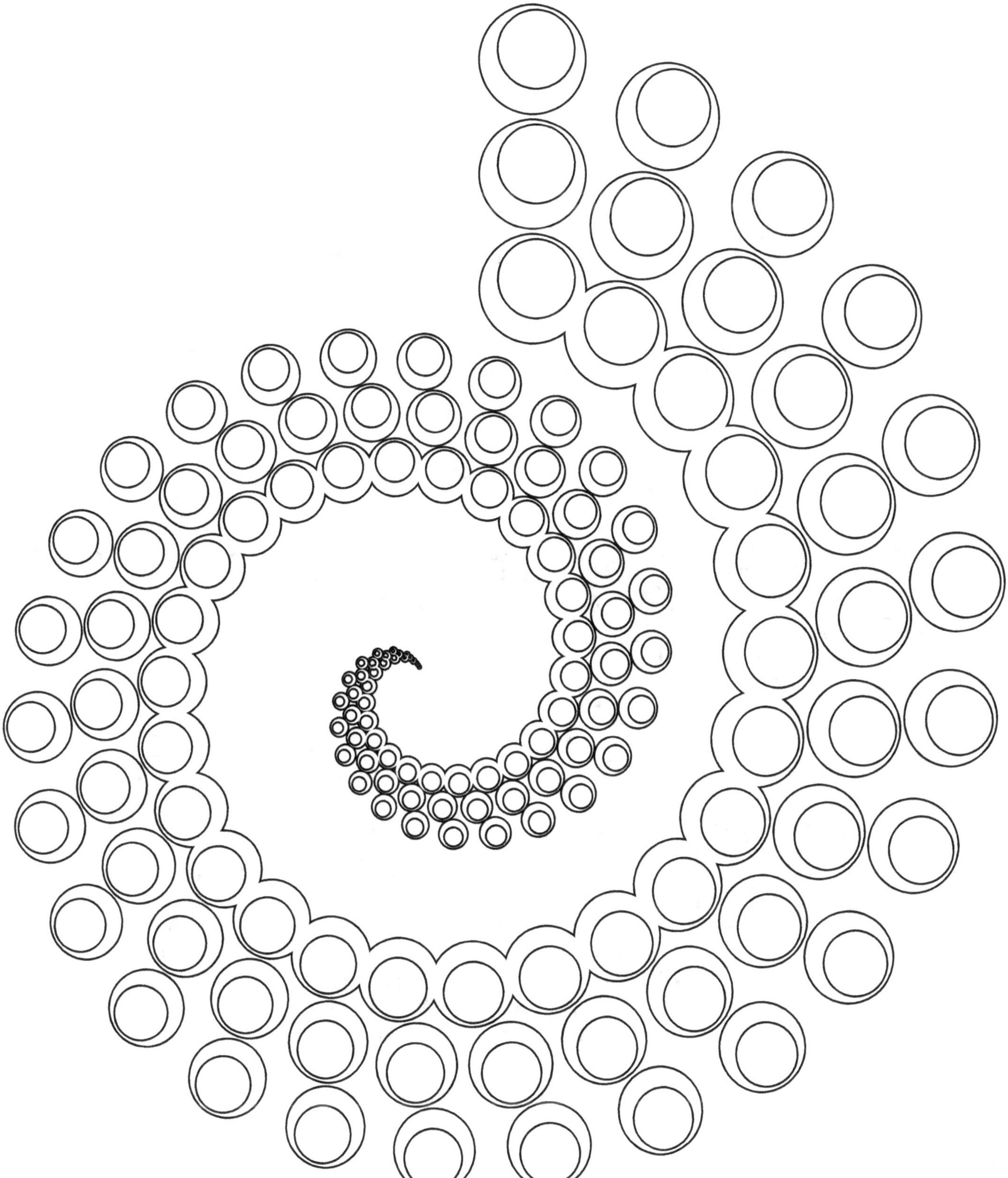

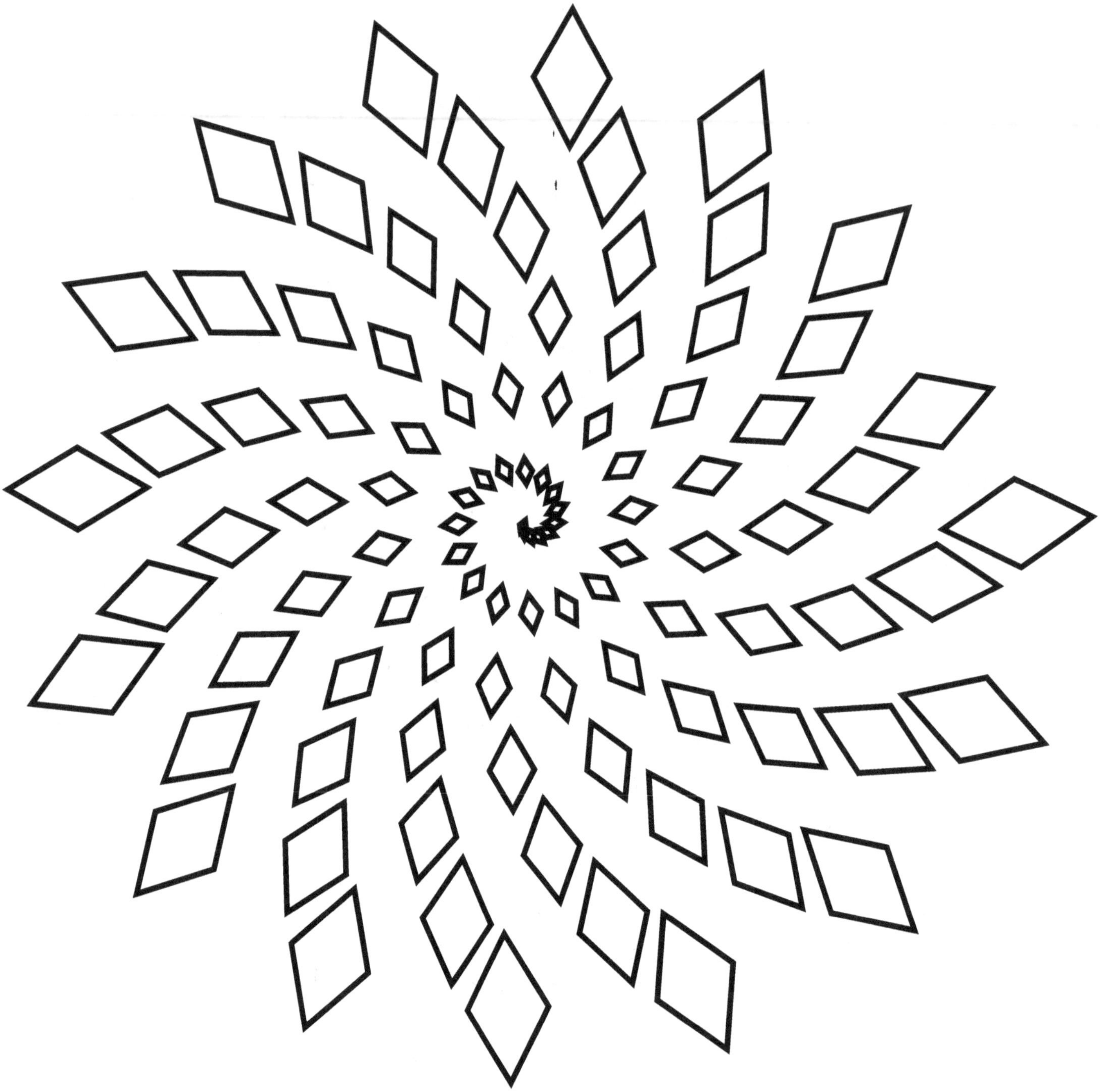

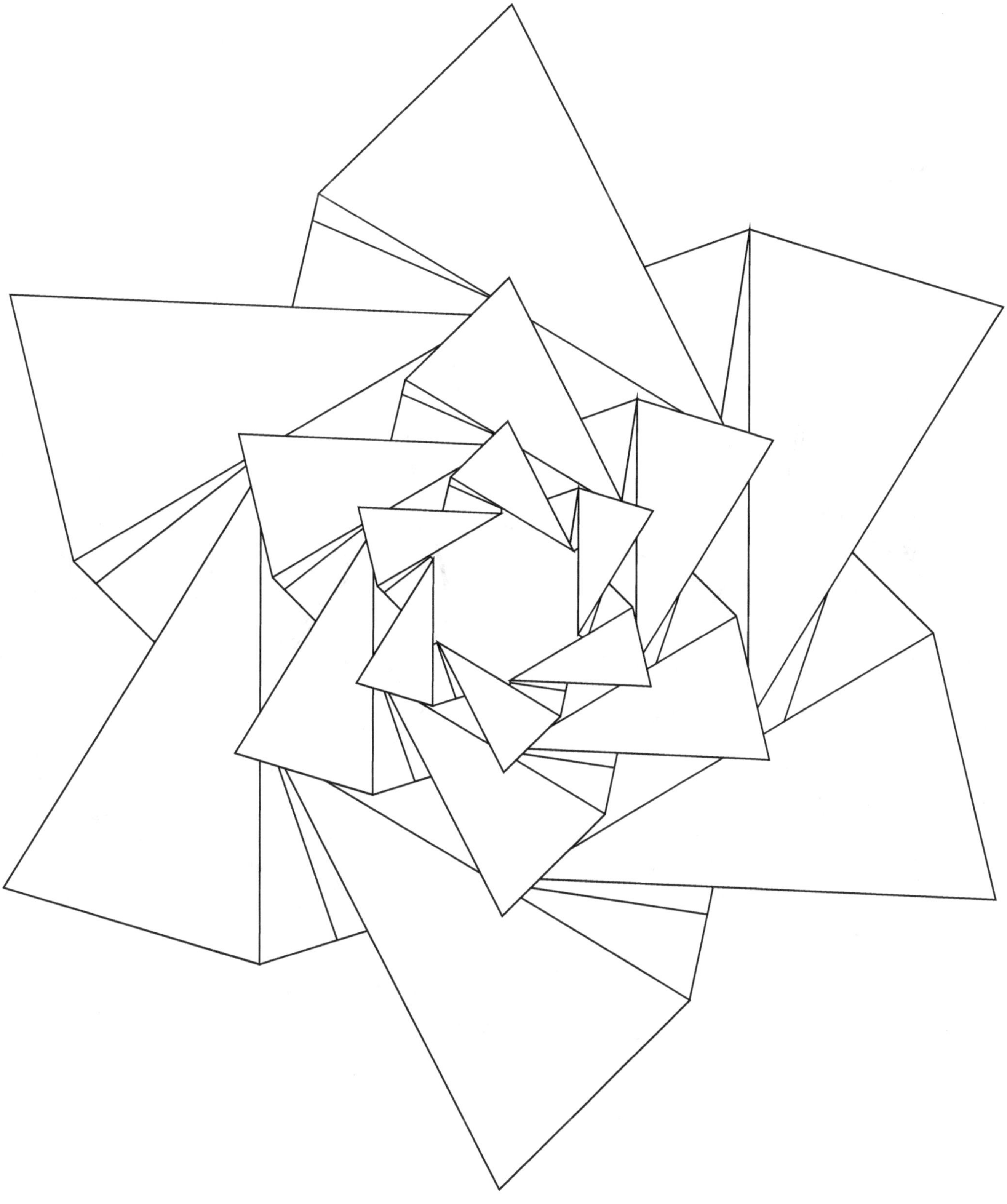

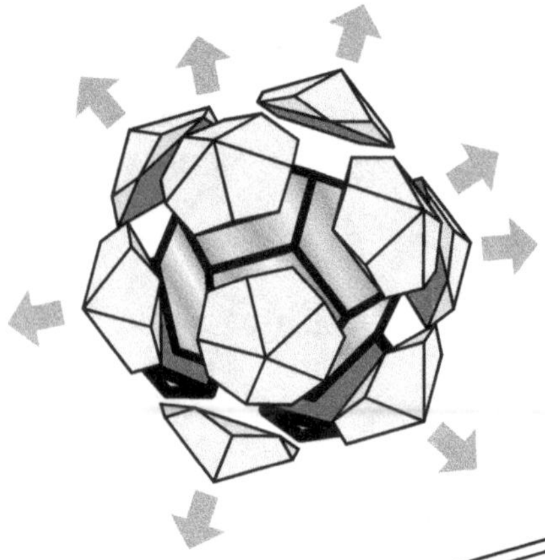

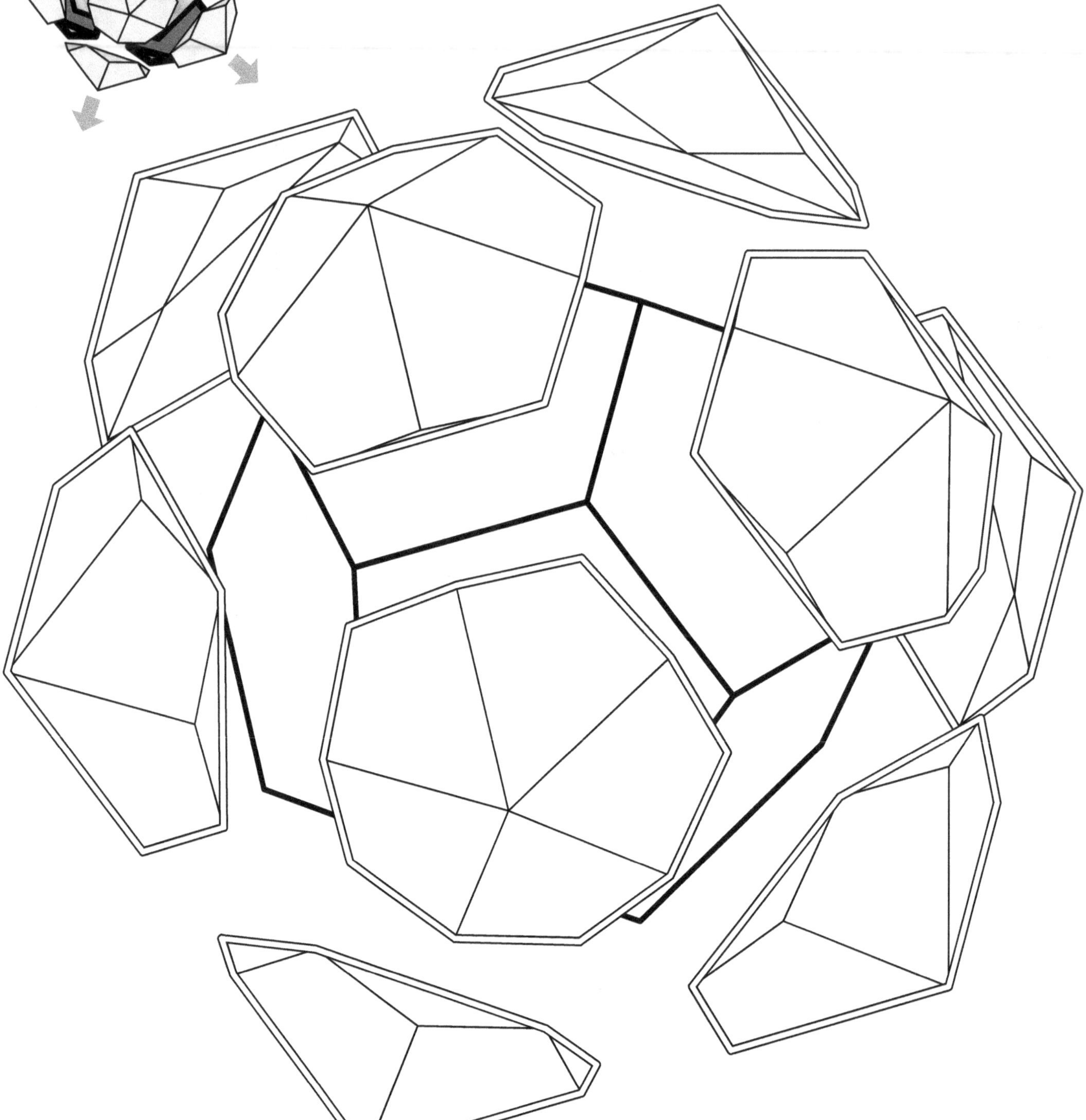

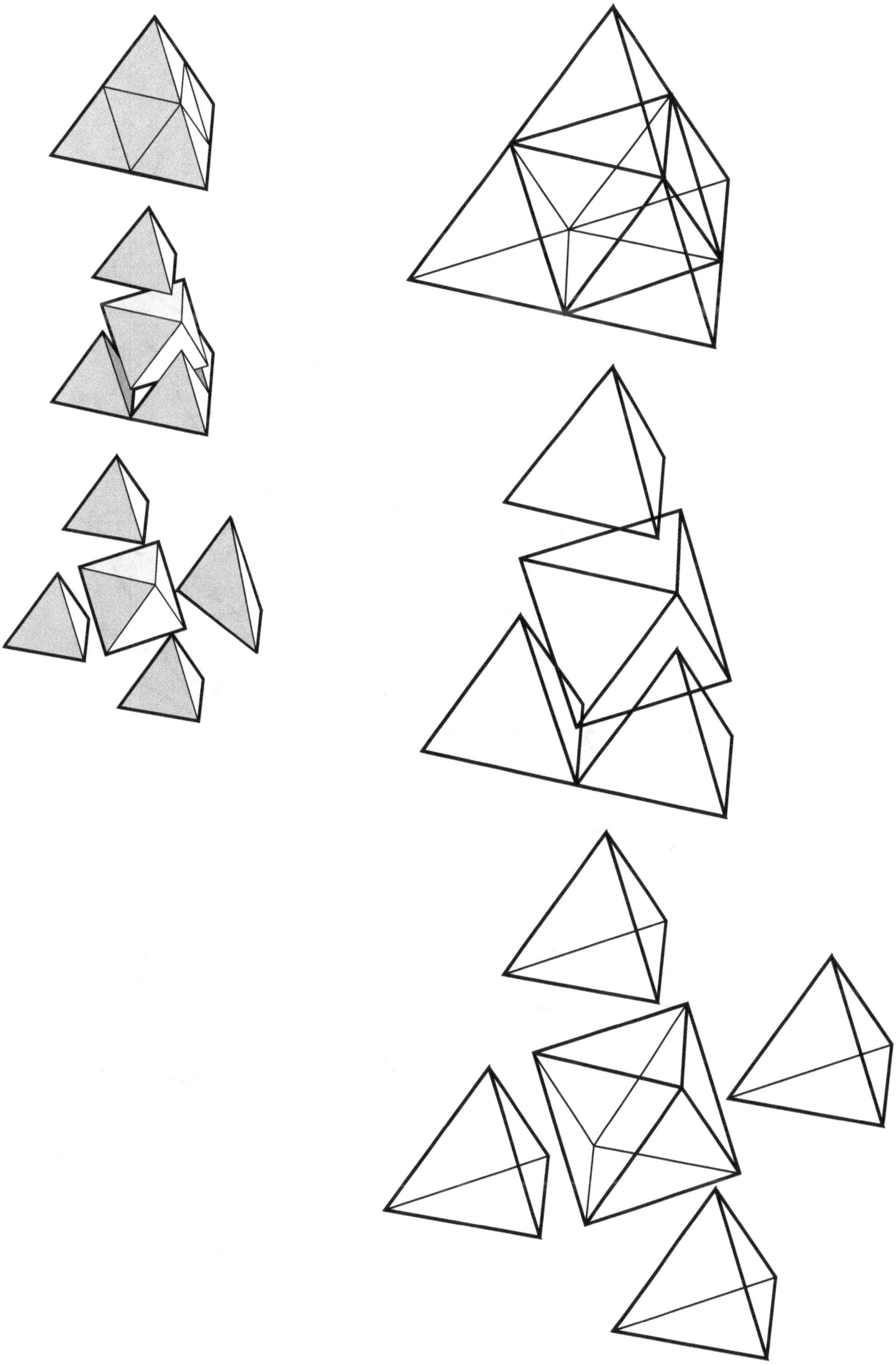

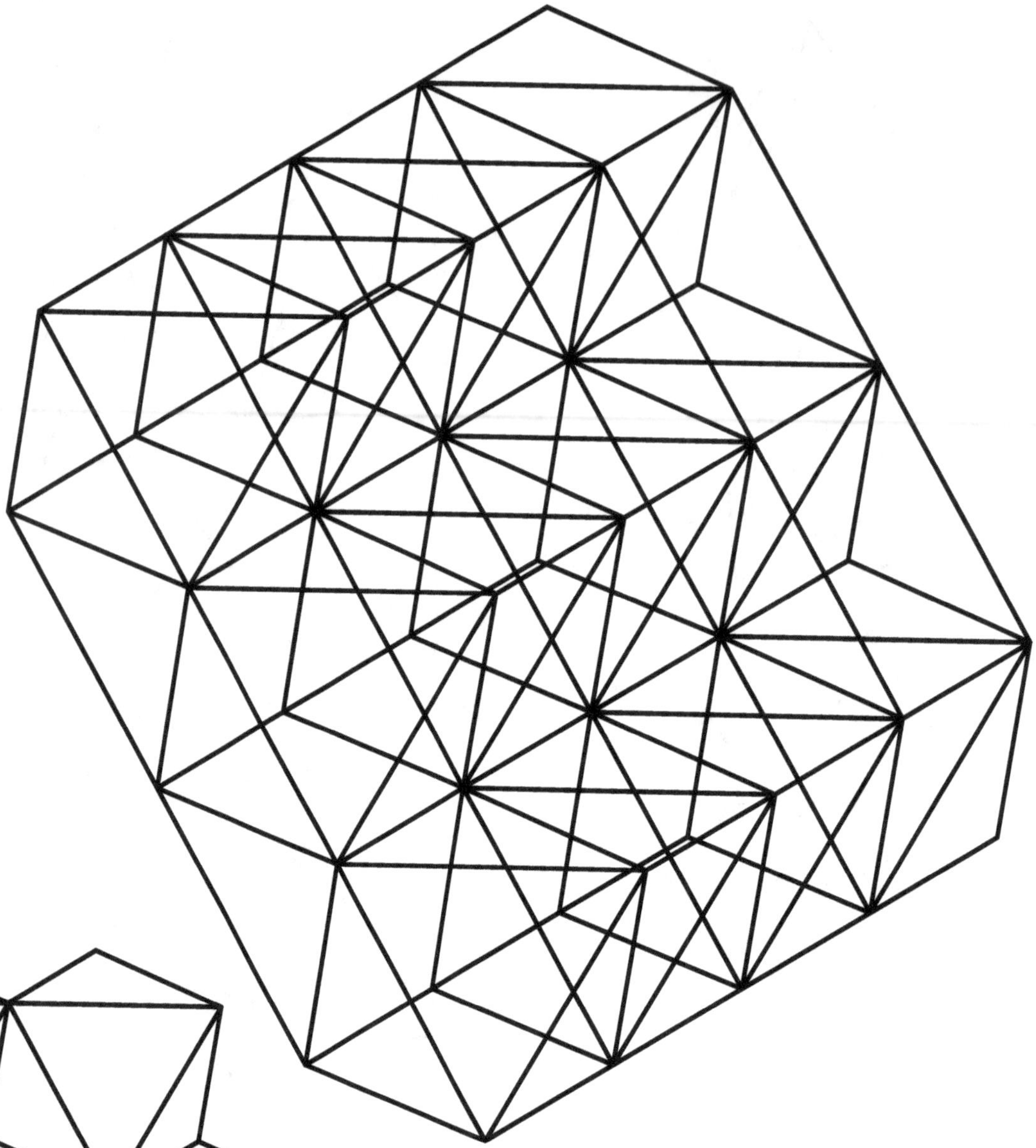

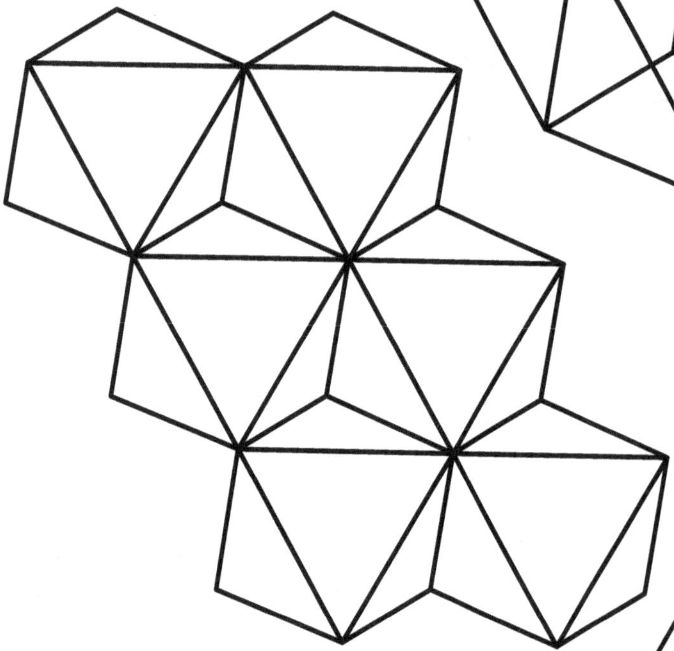

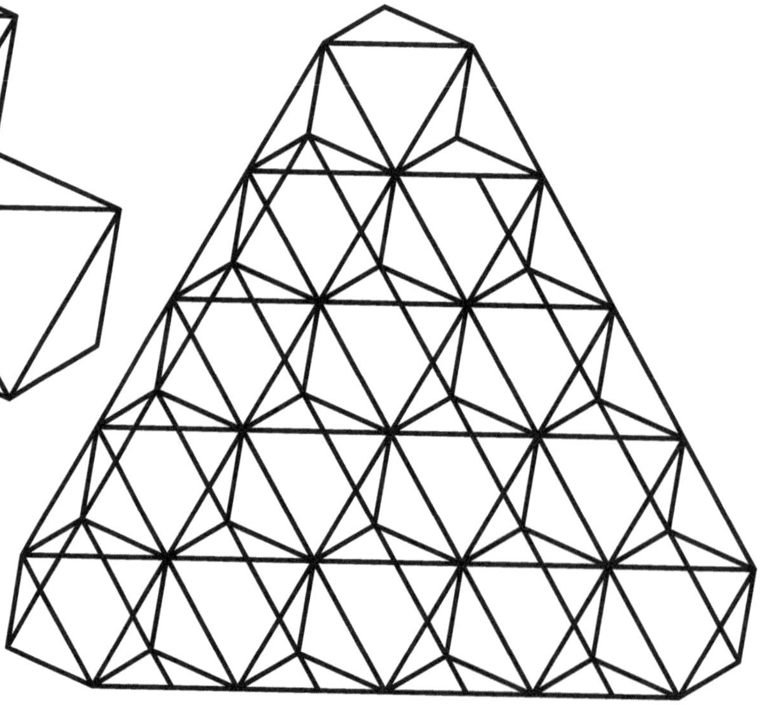

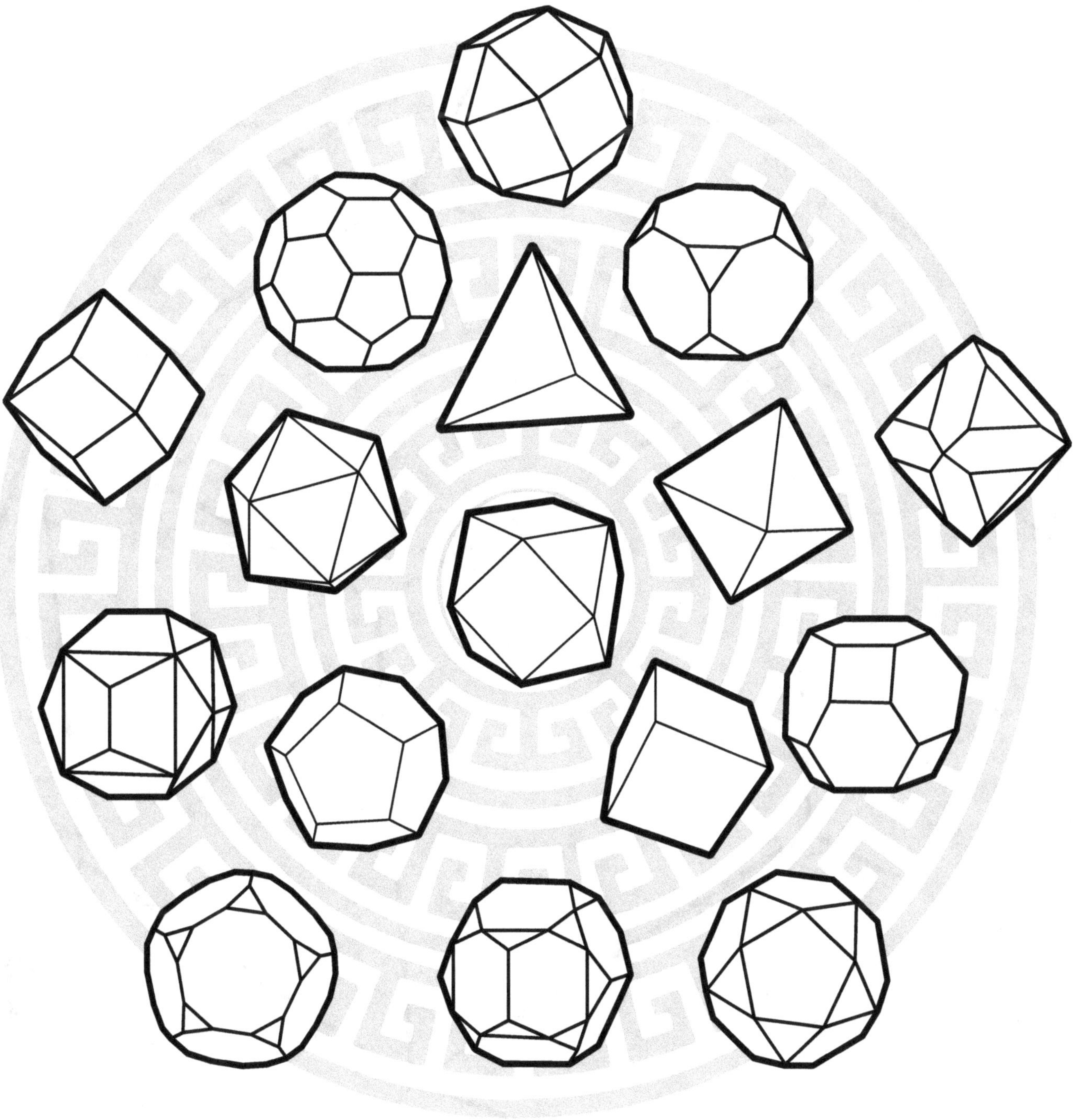

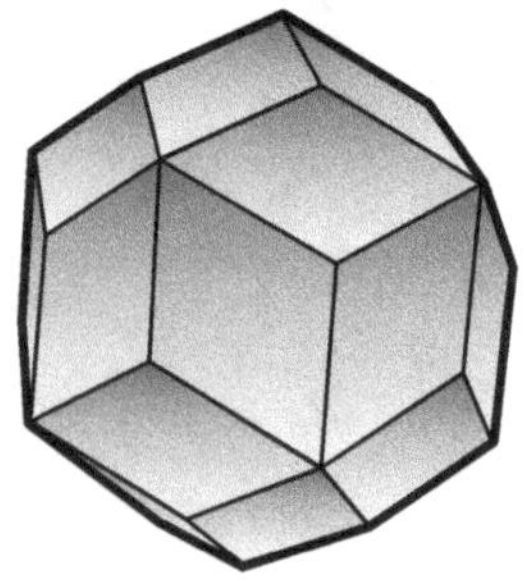

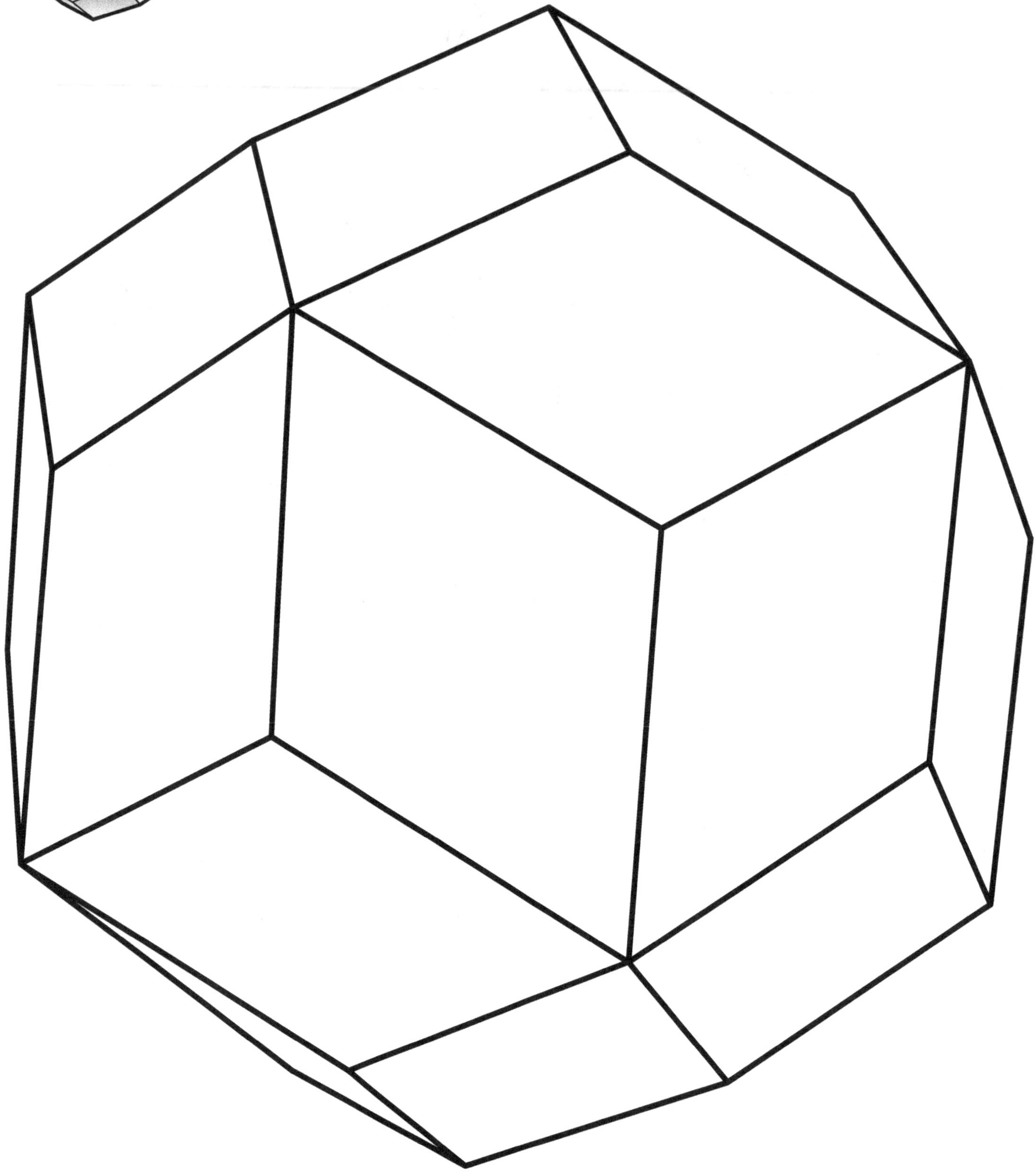

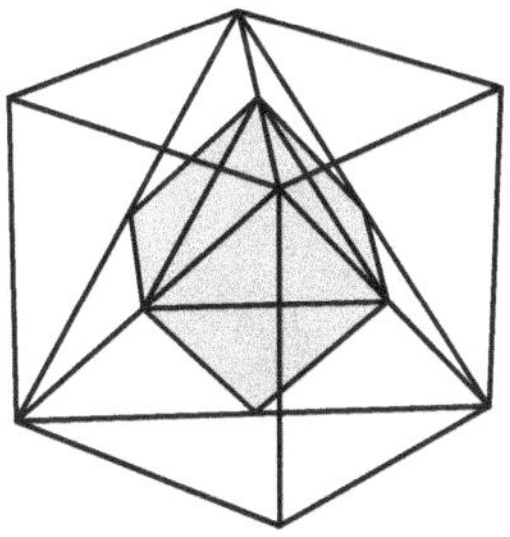
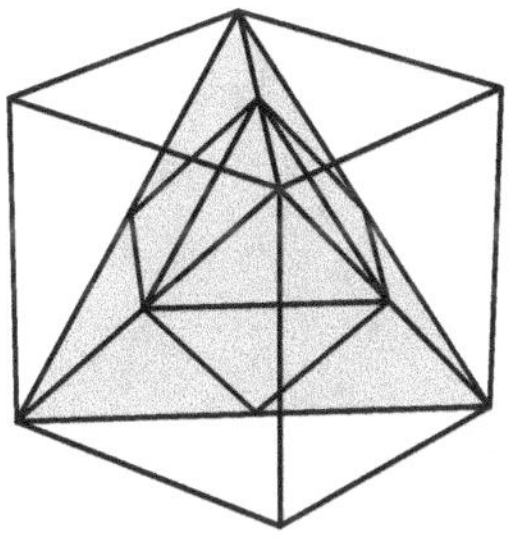
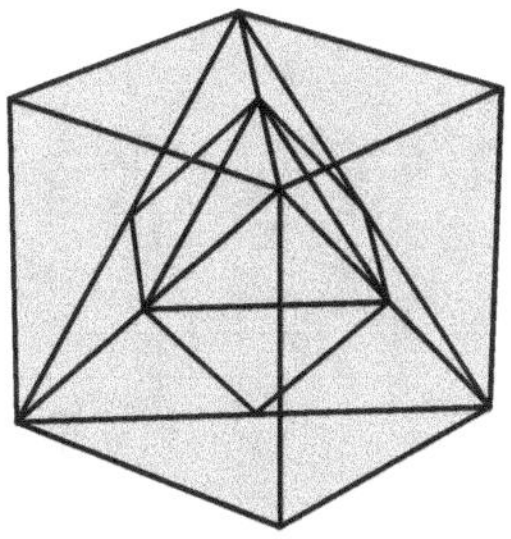
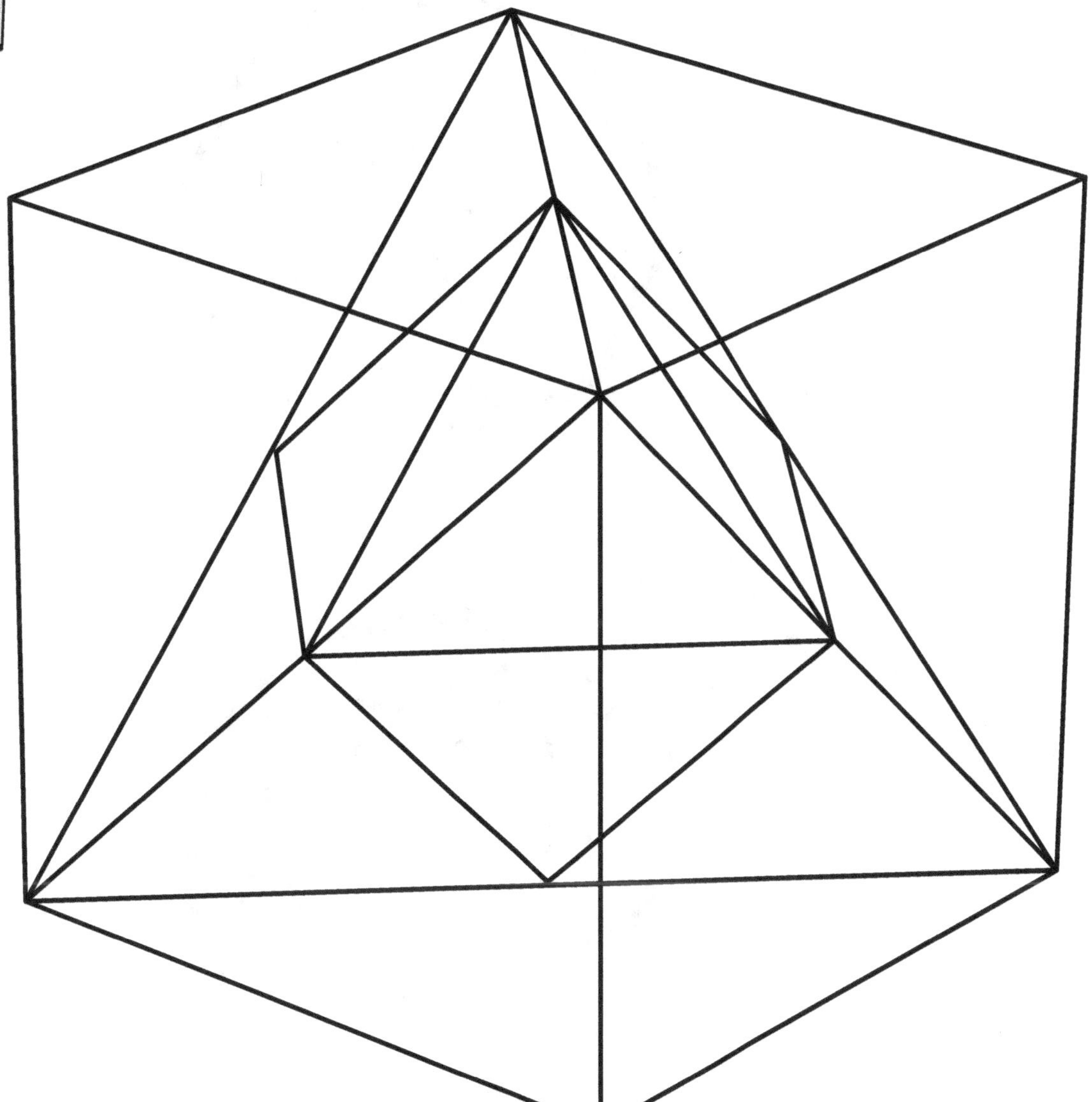

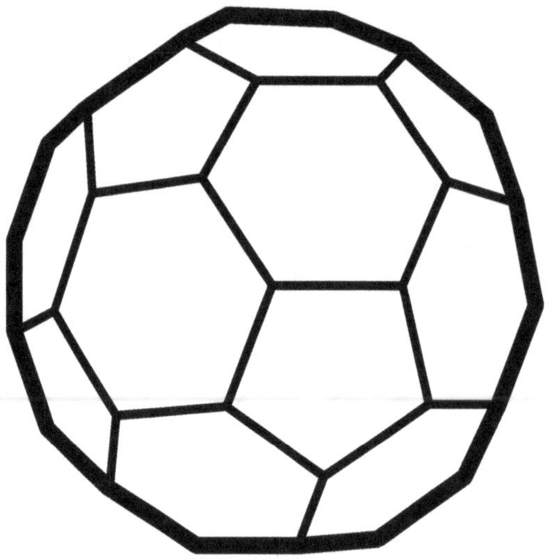

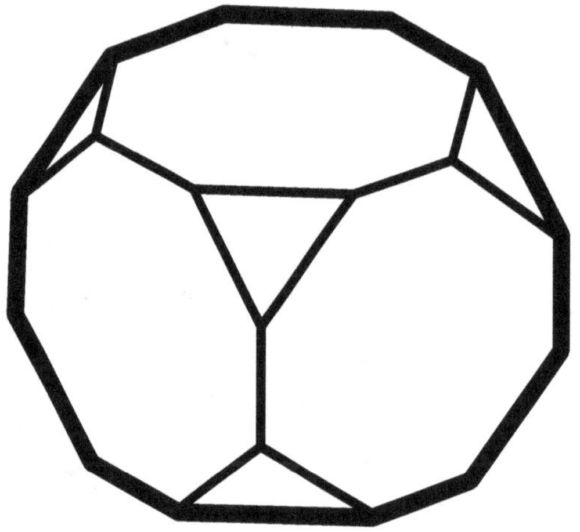

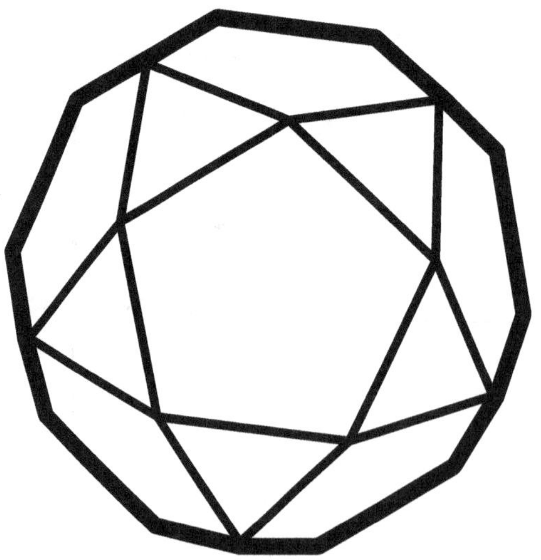

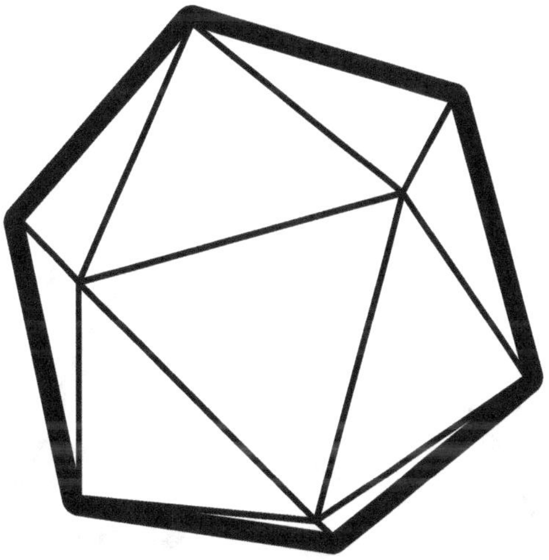
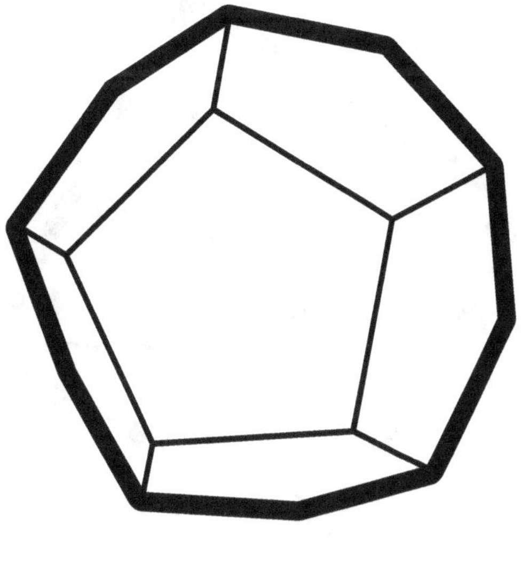
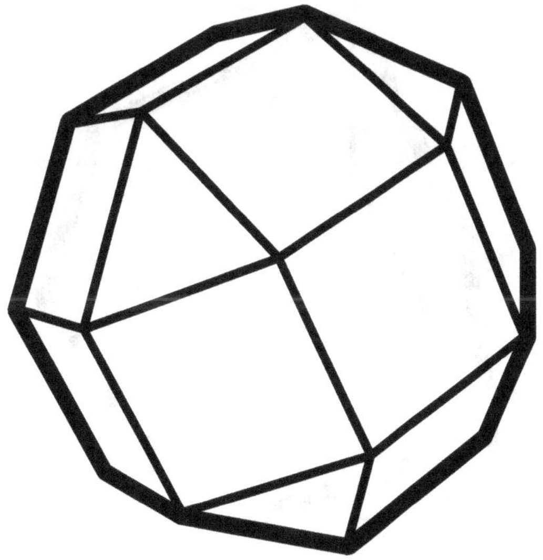

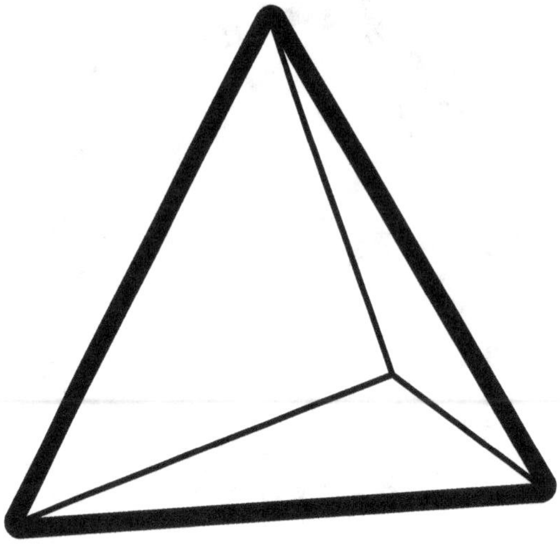

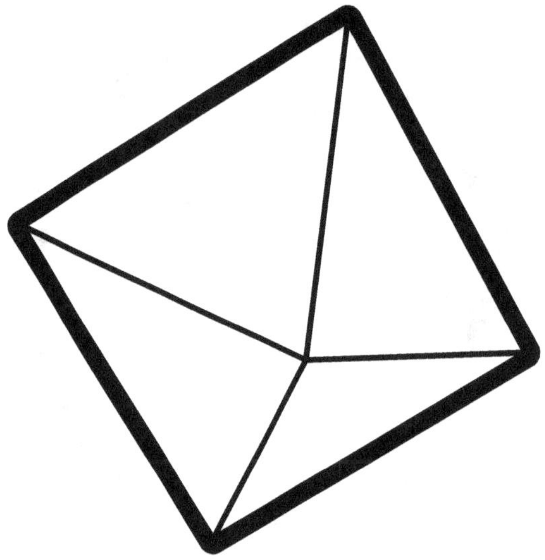

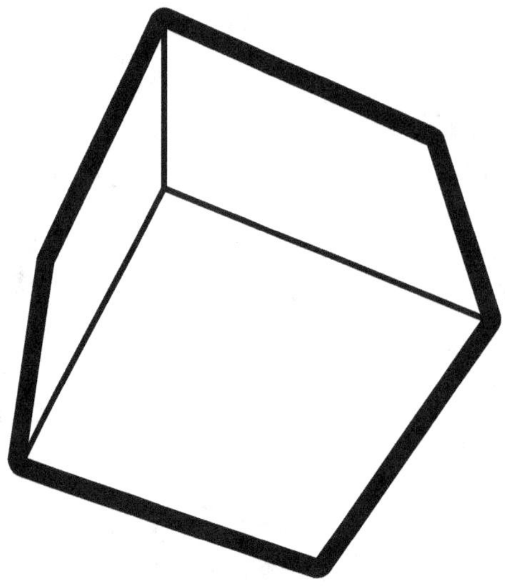

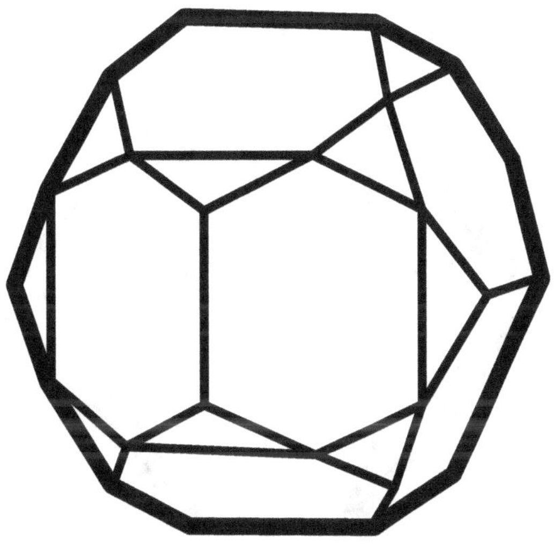

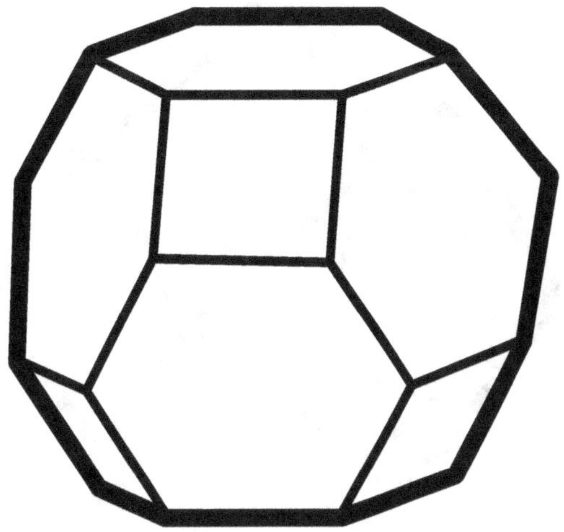

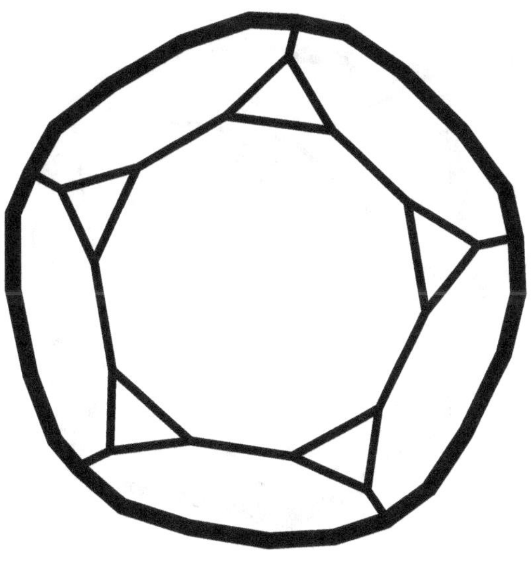

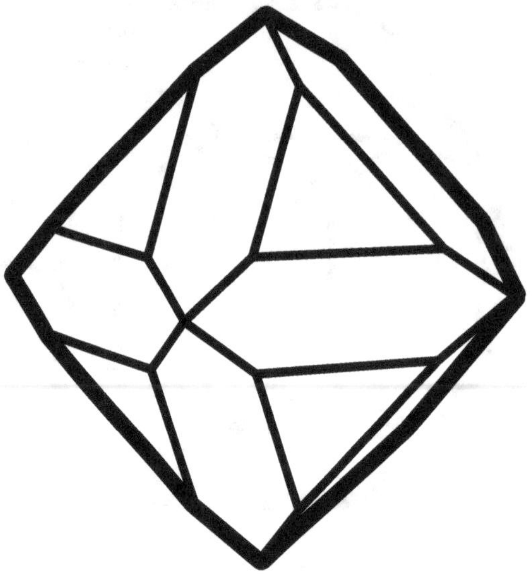

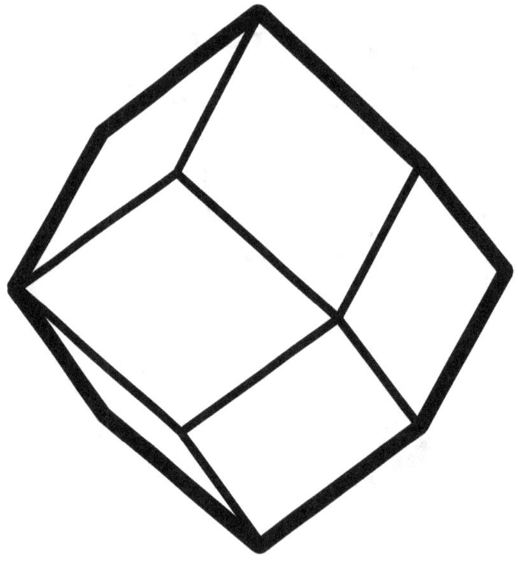

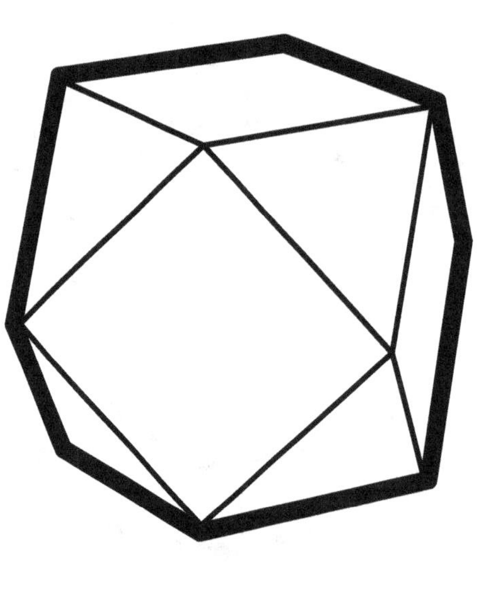

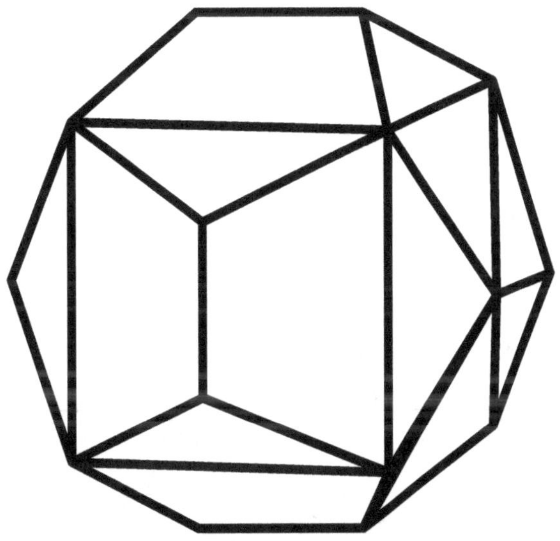

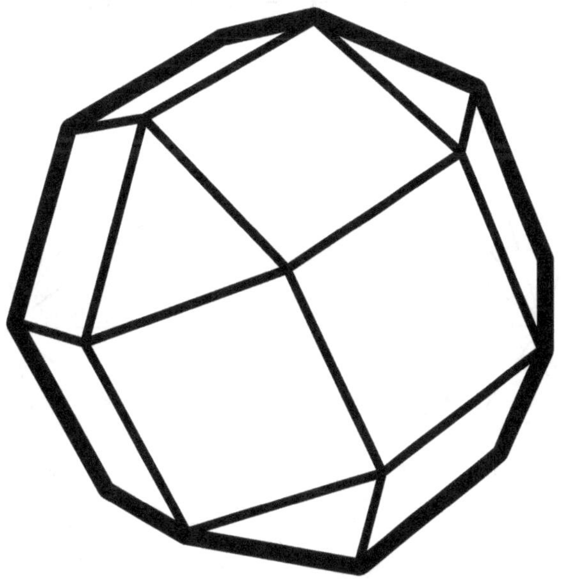

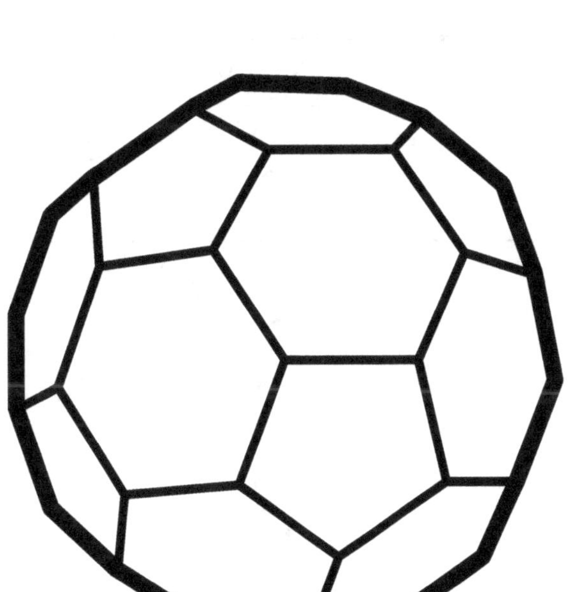

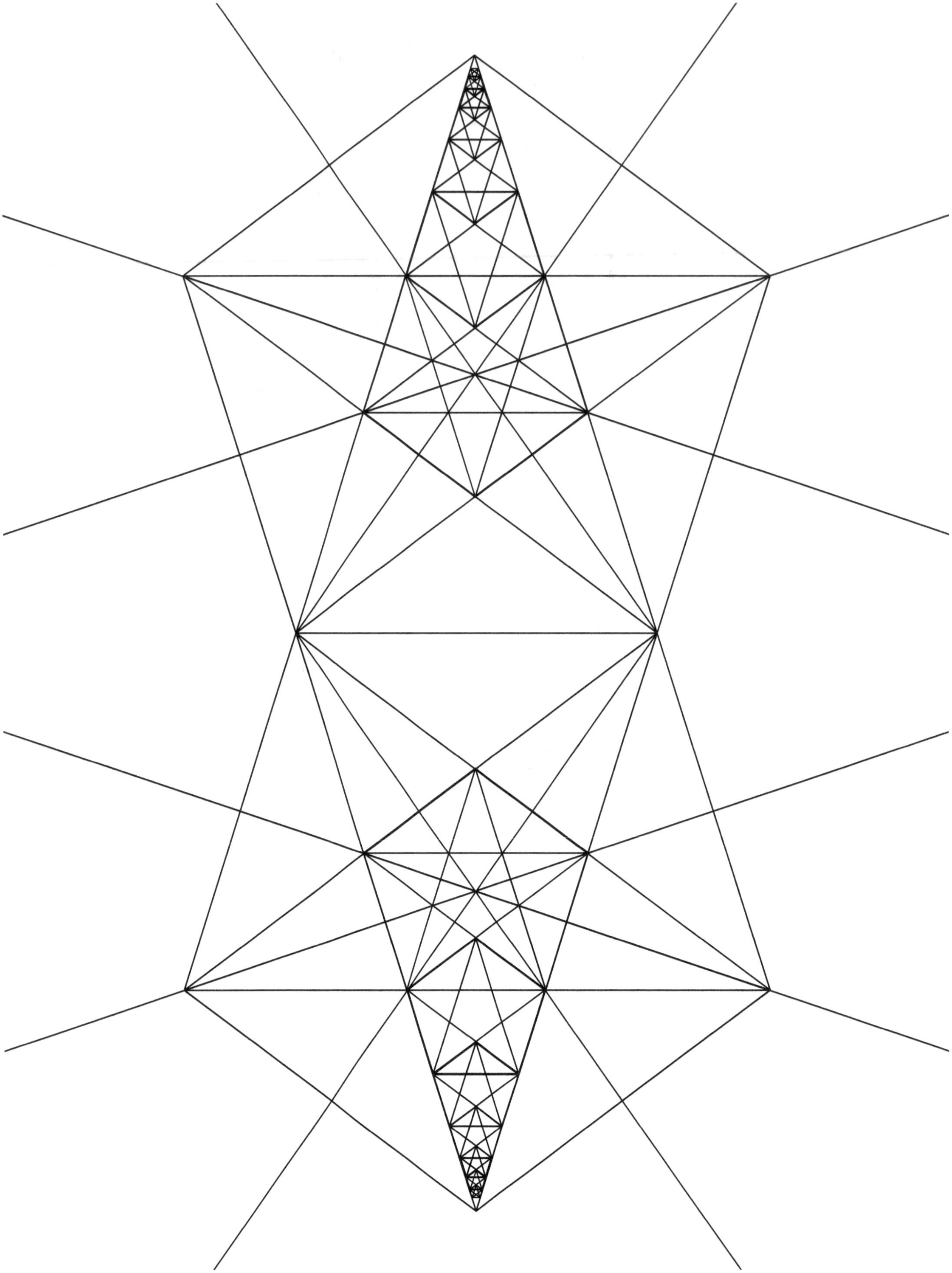

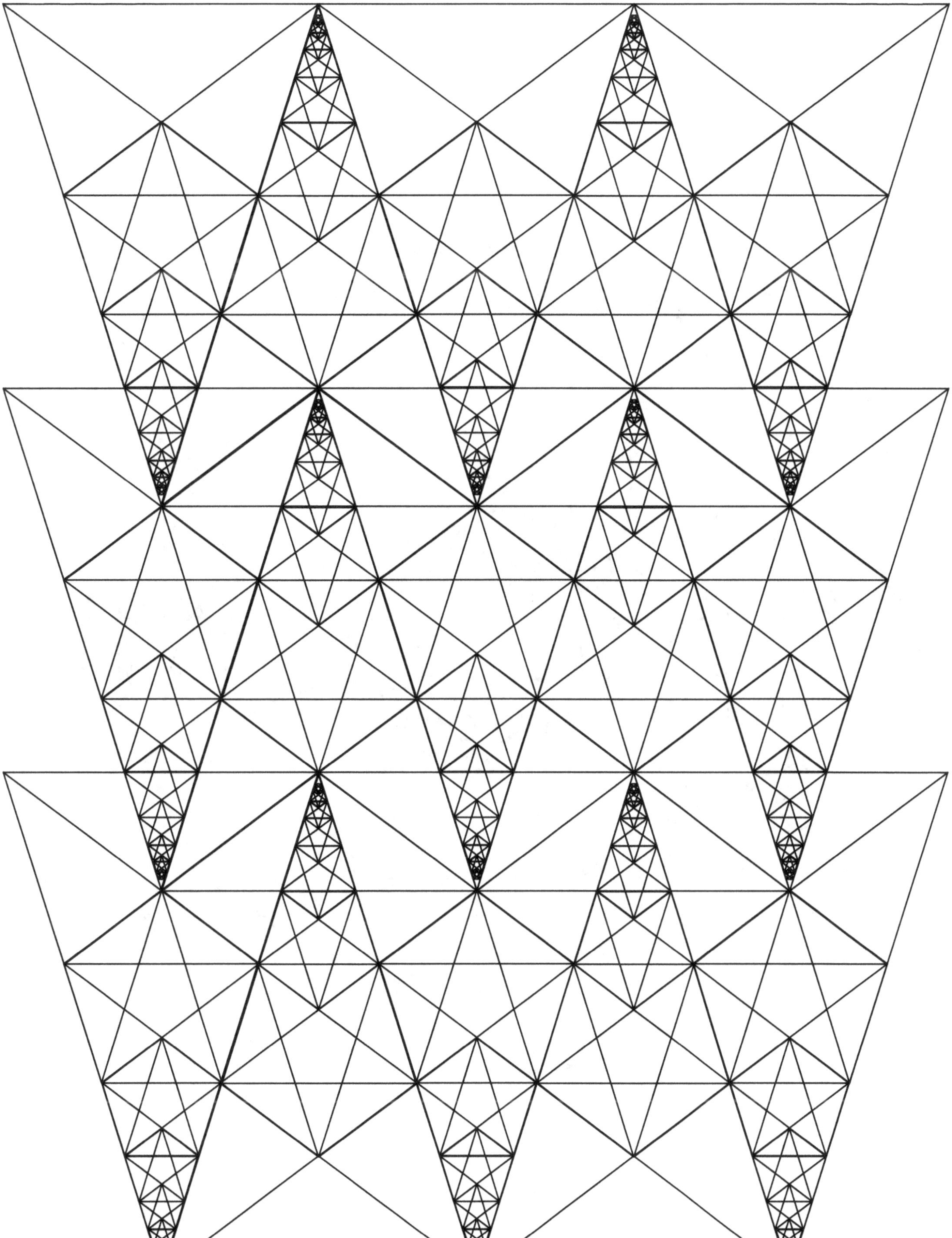

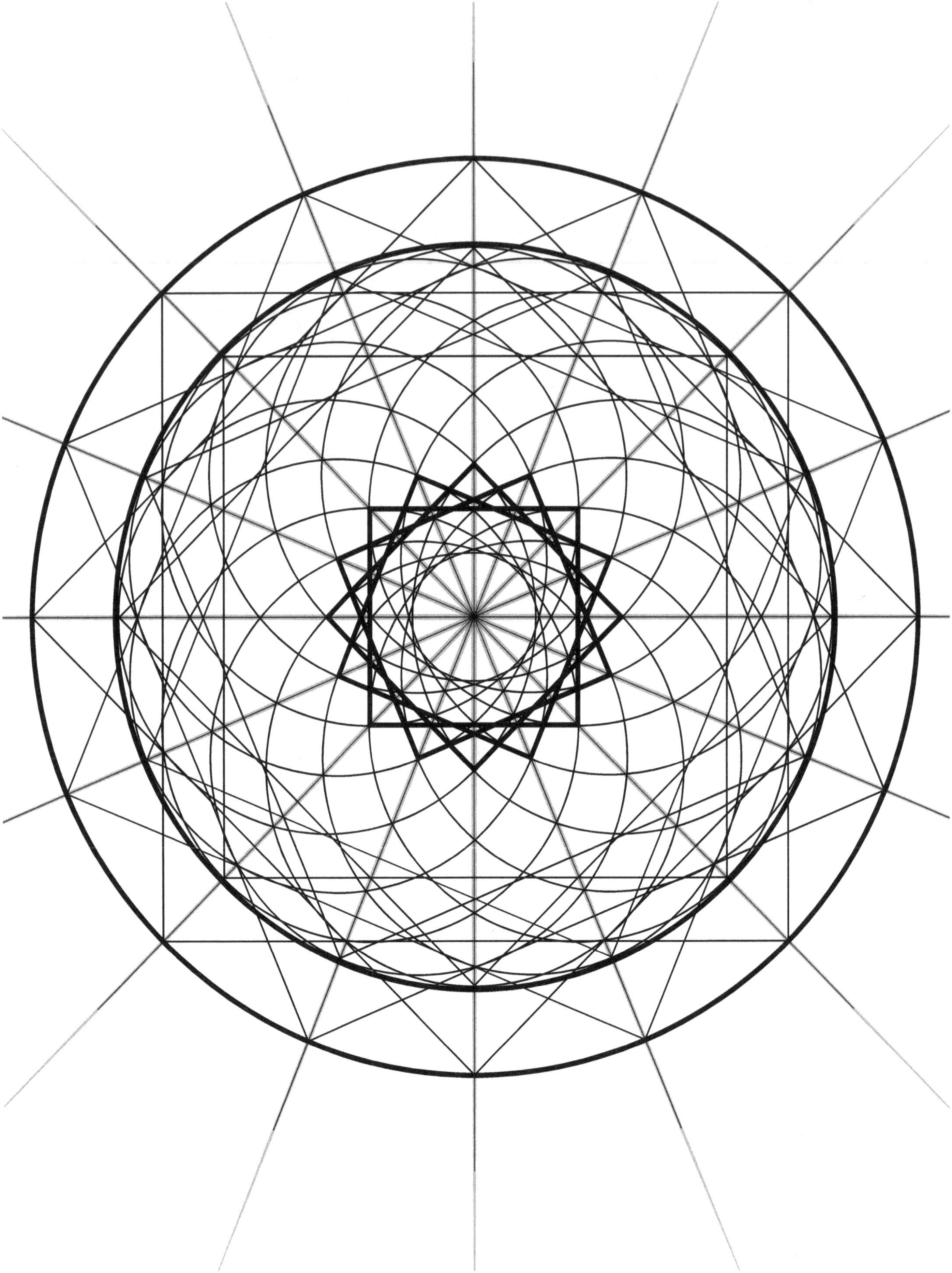

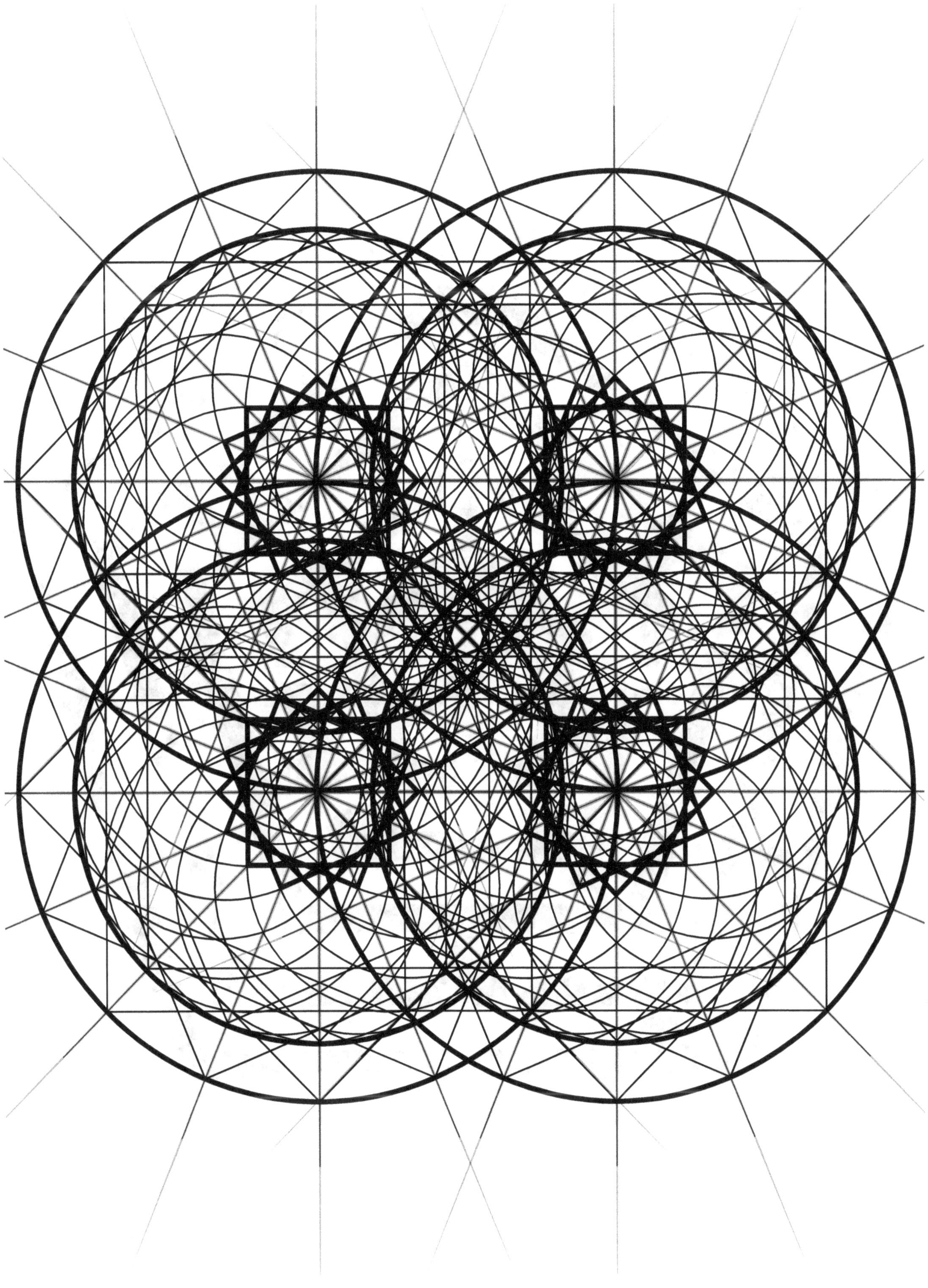

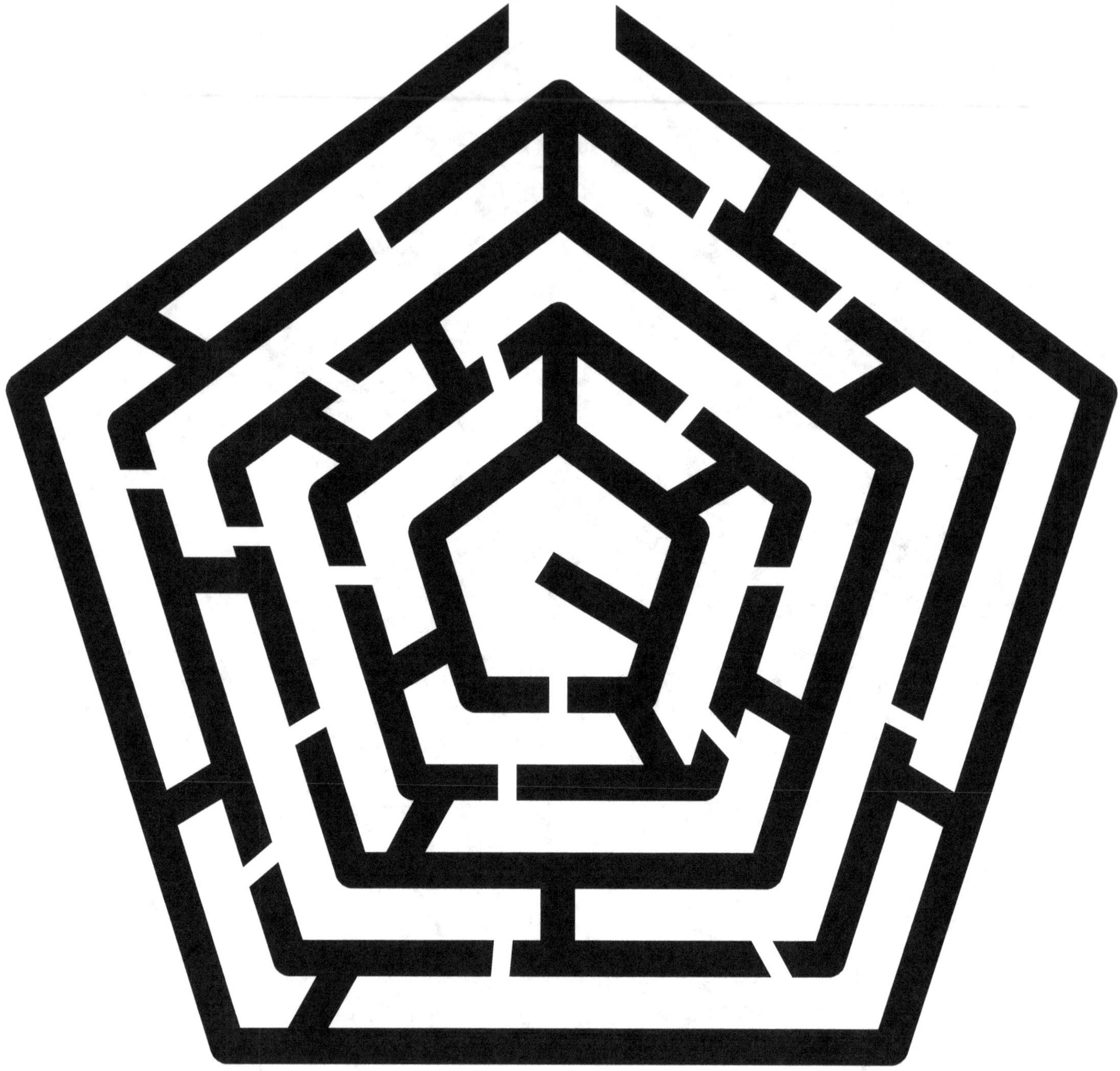

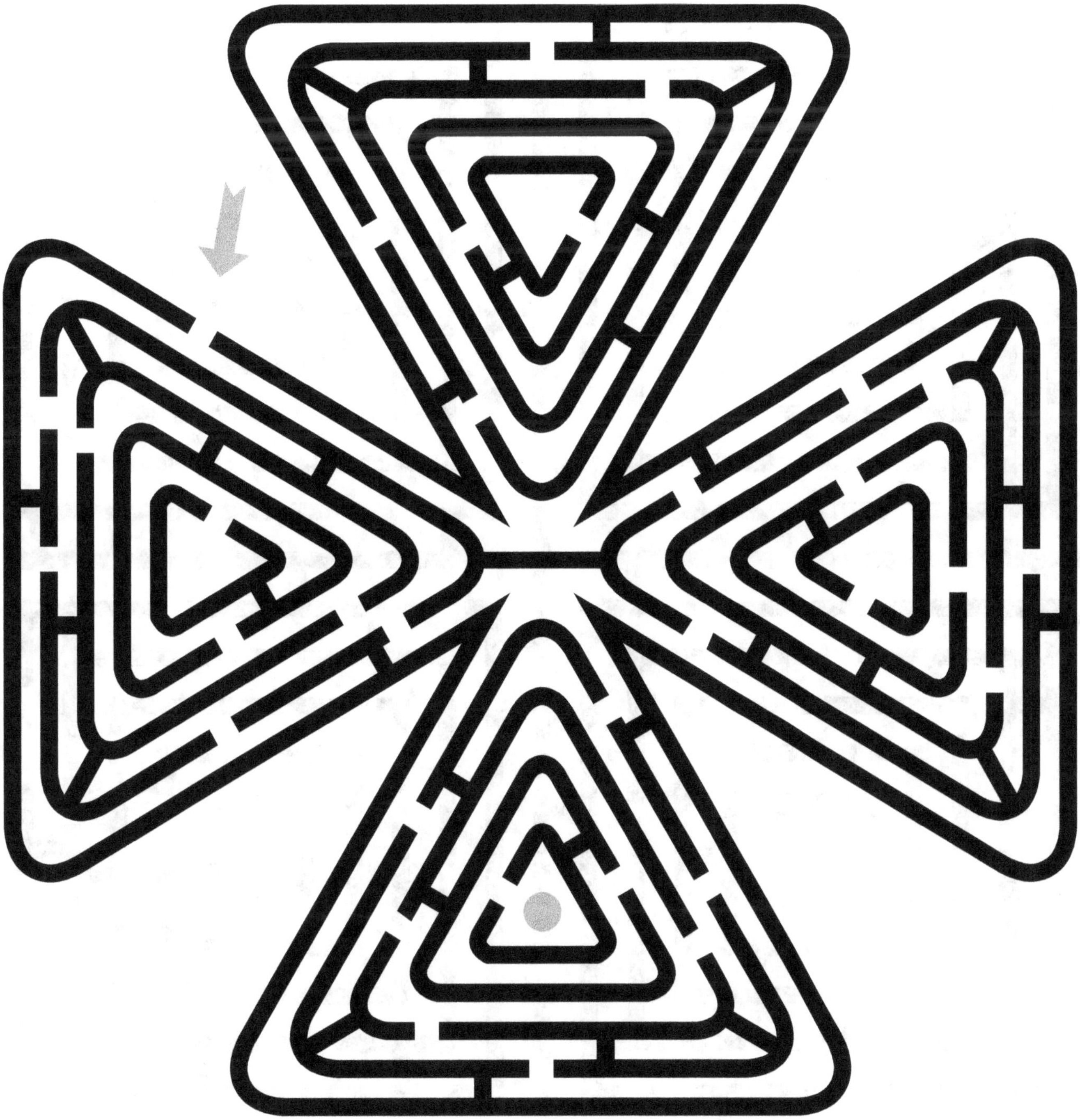

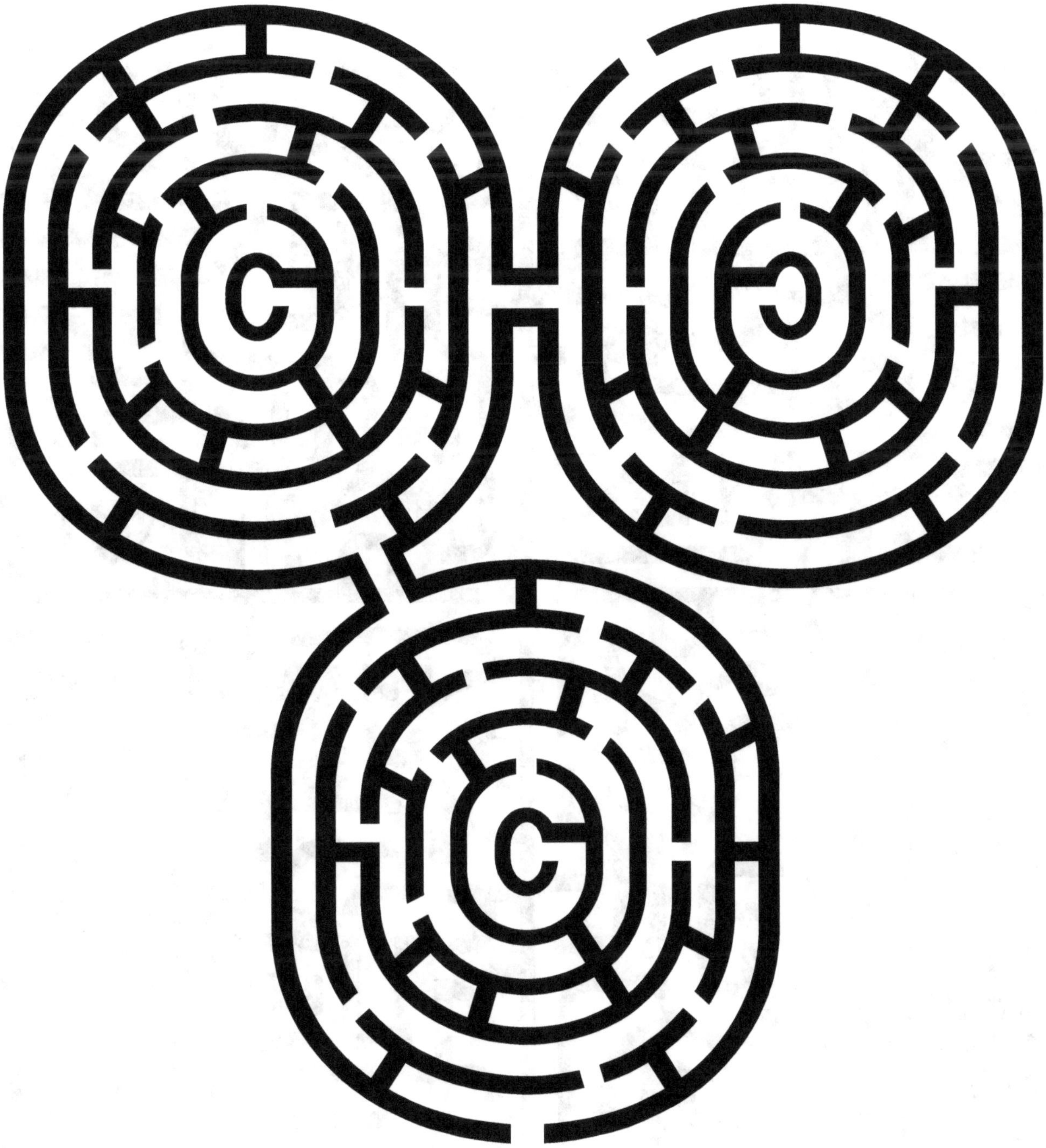

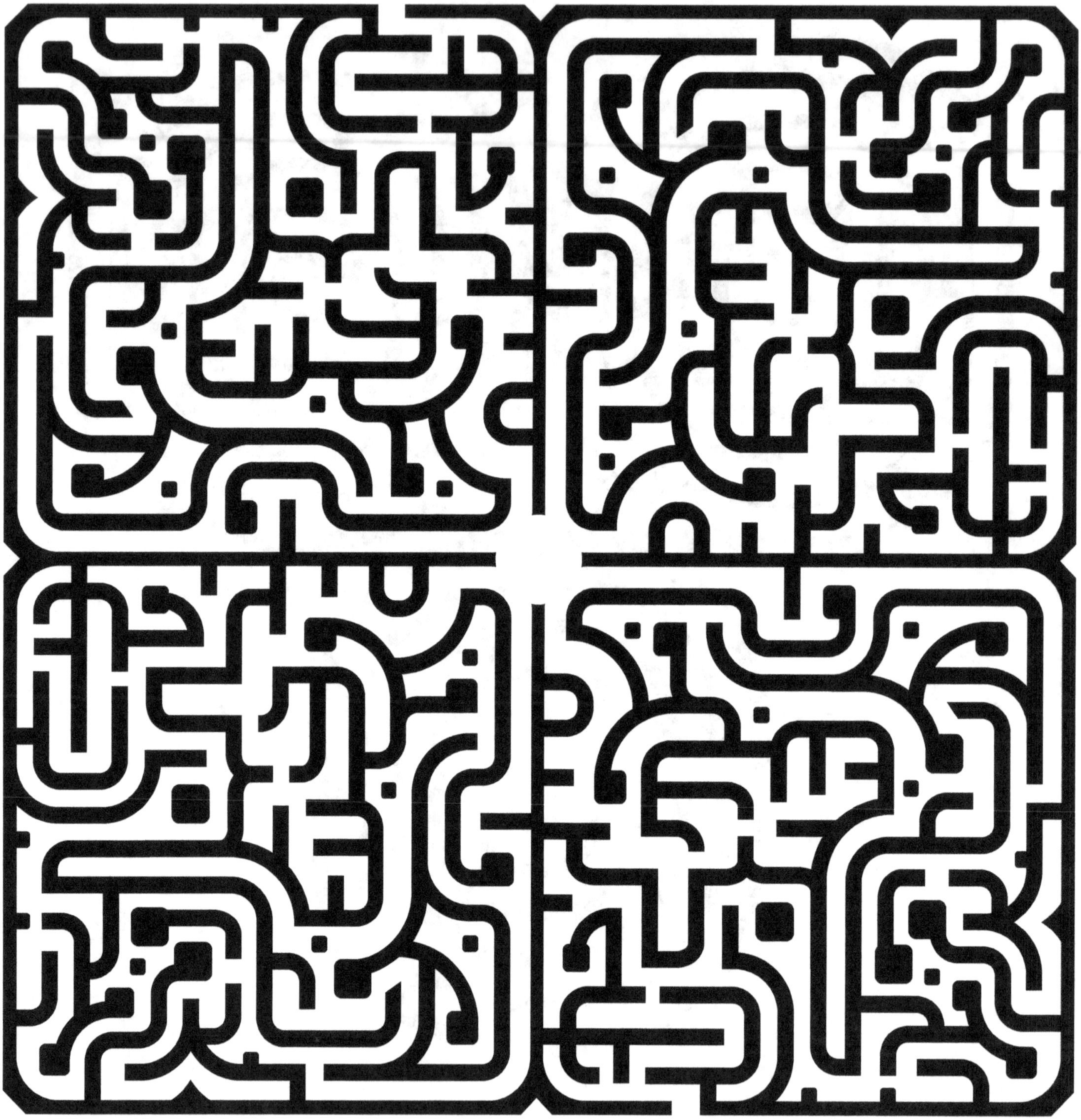

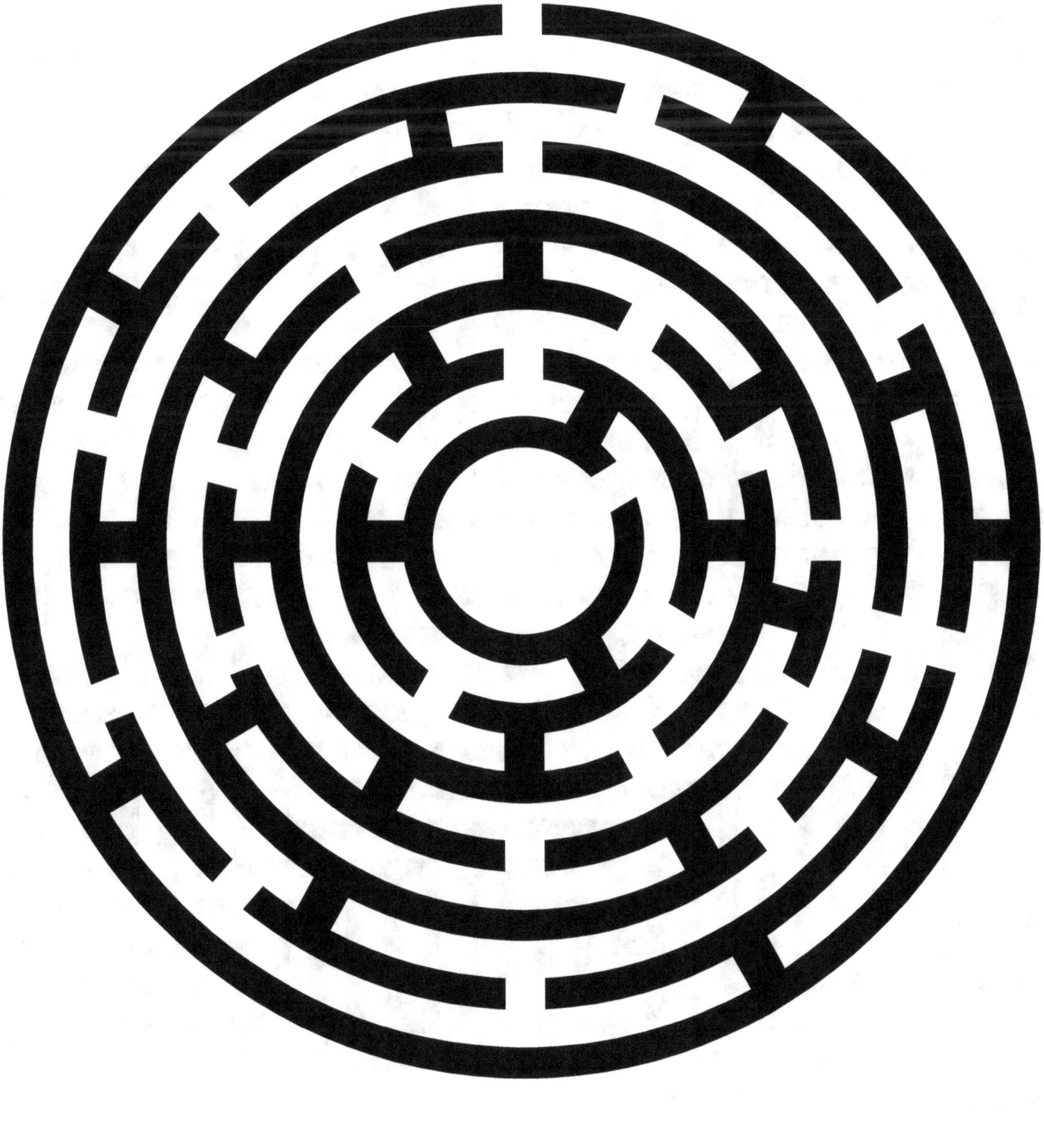

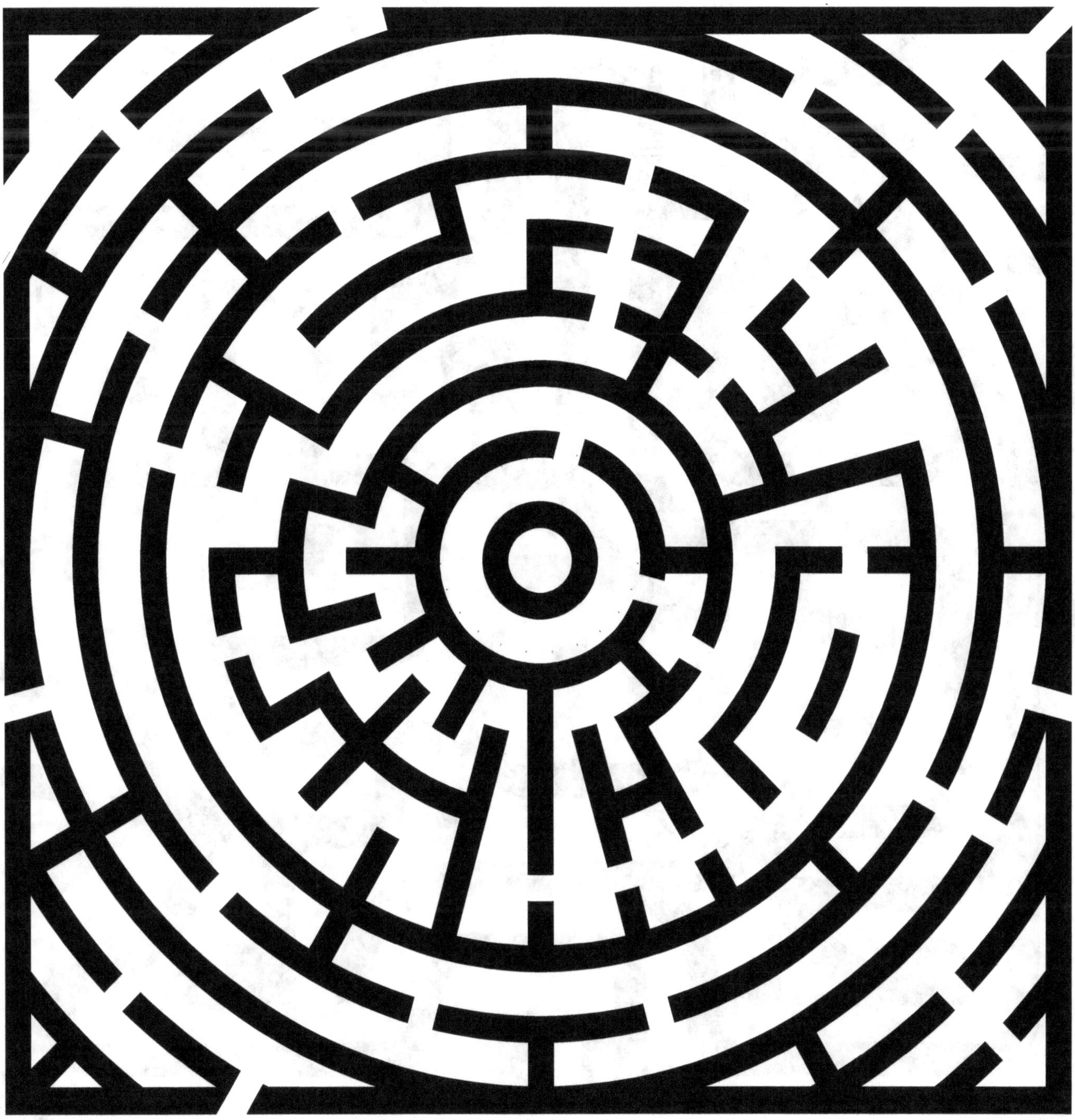

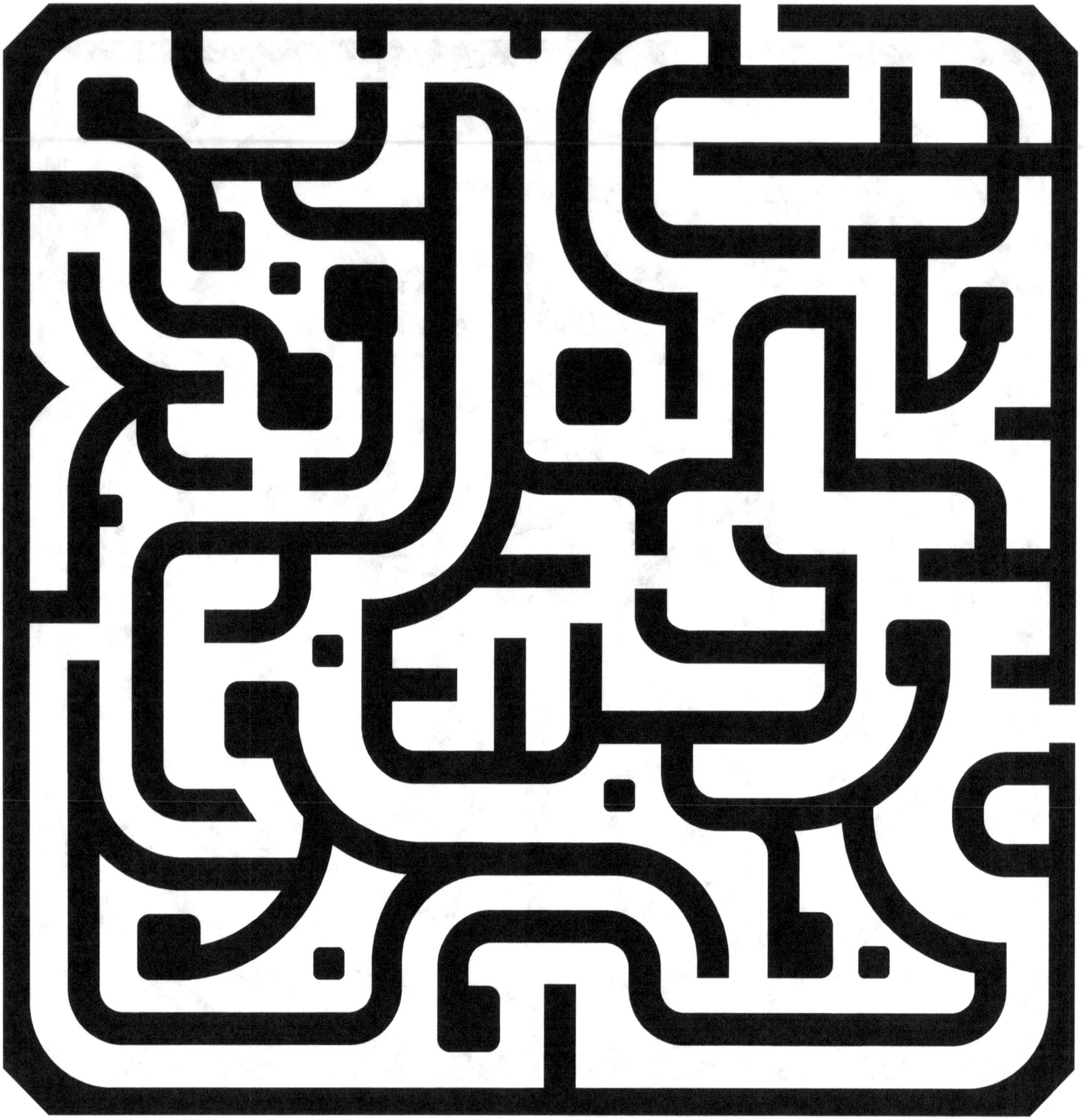

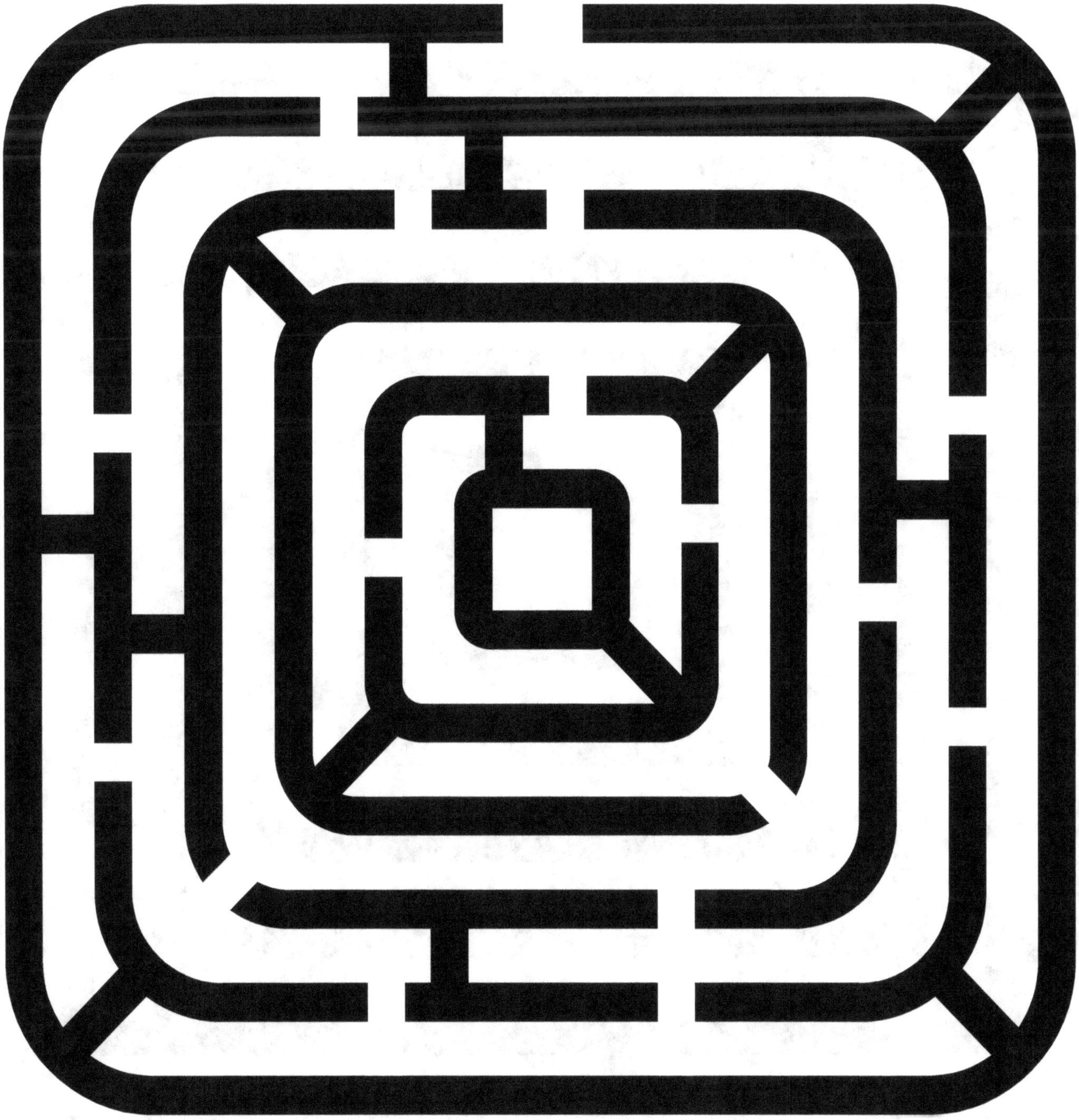

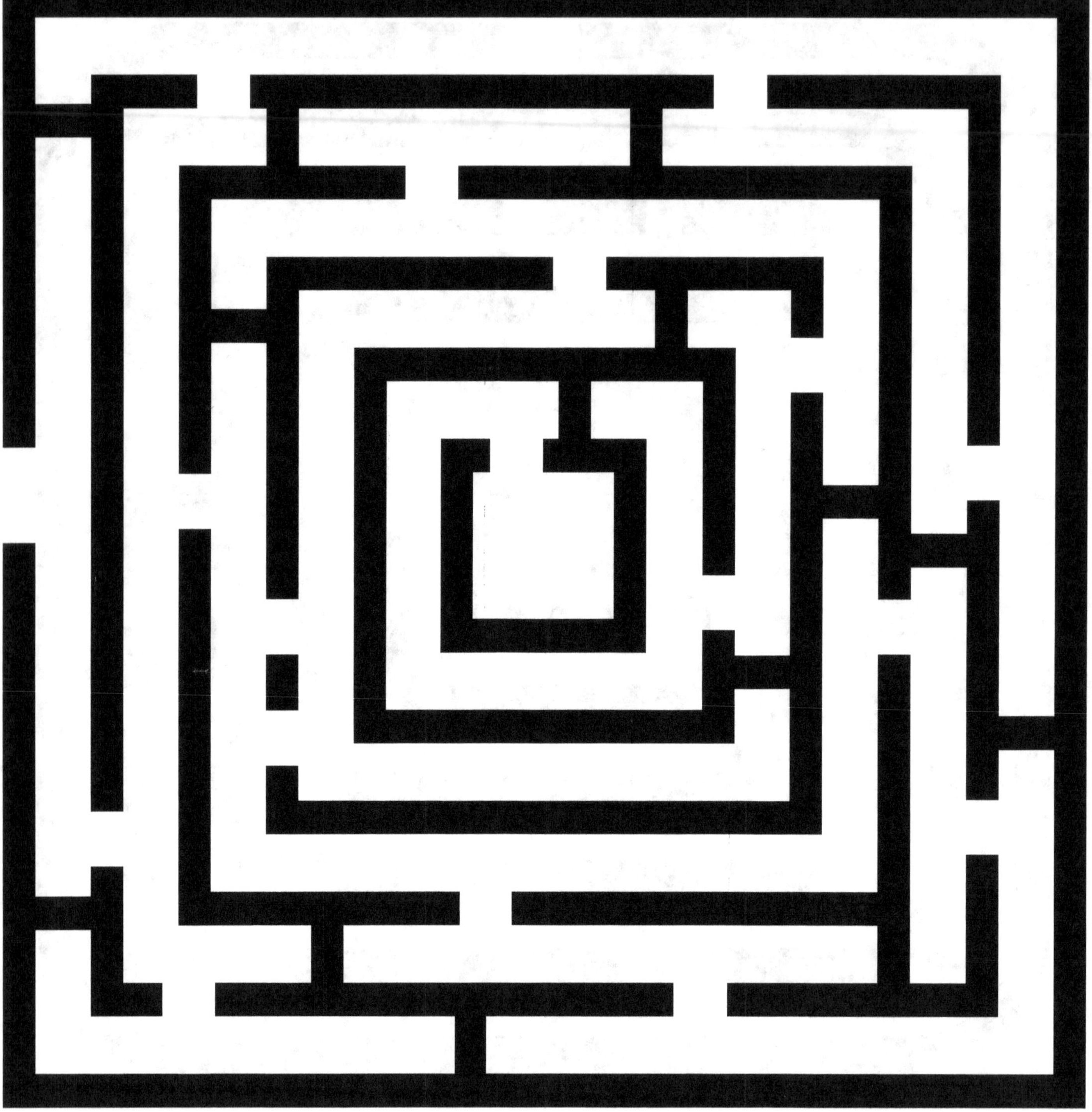

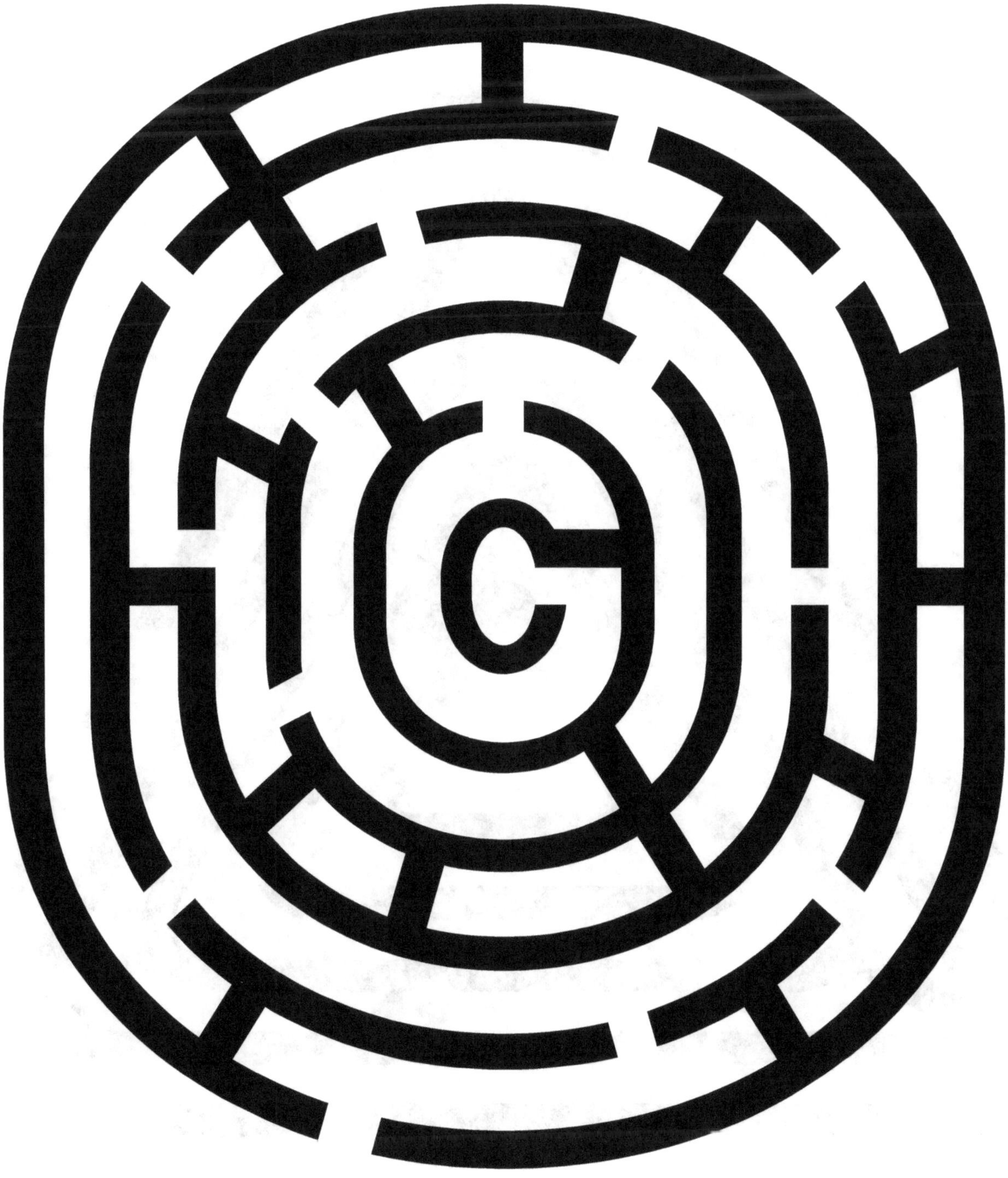
C

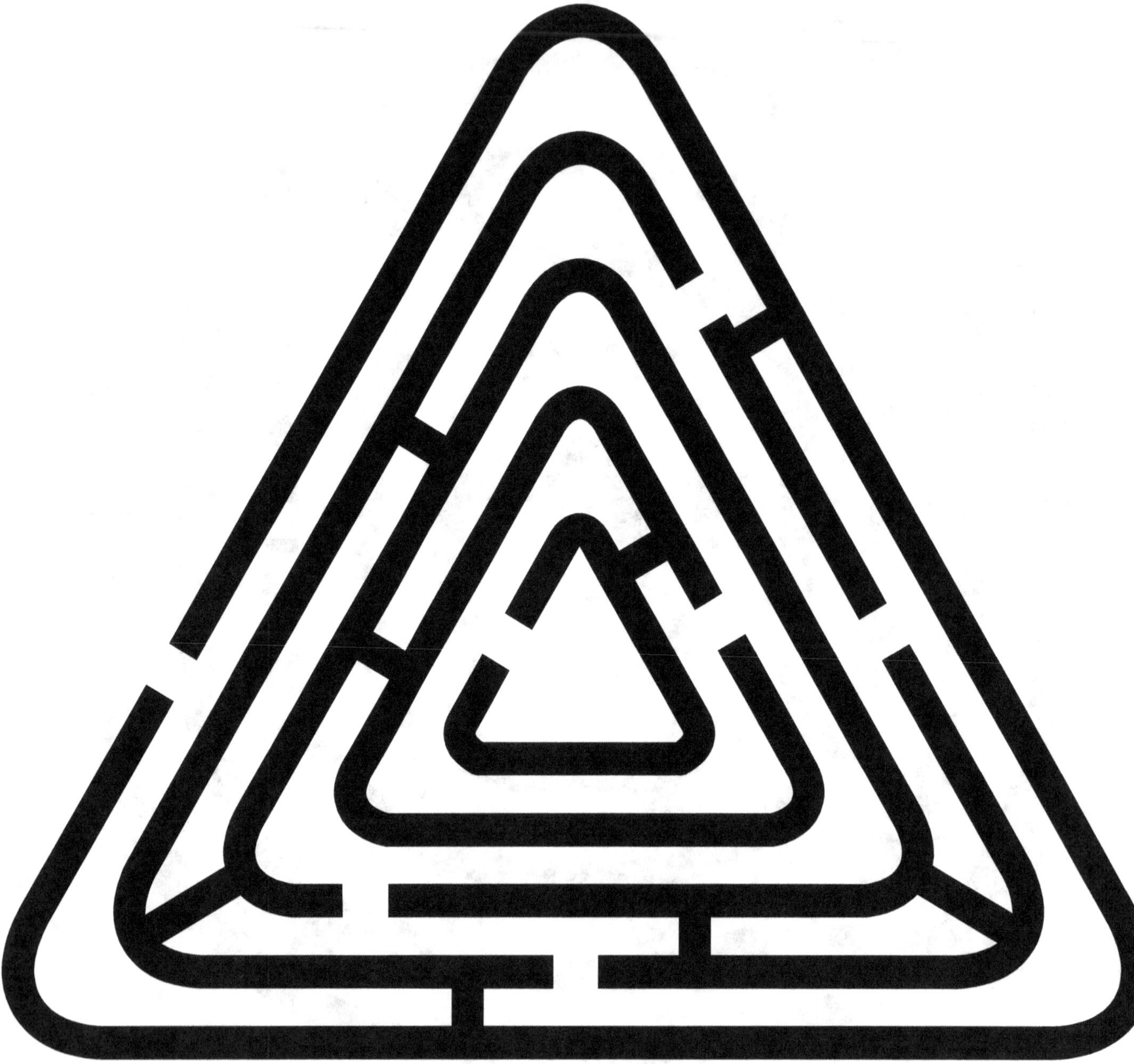

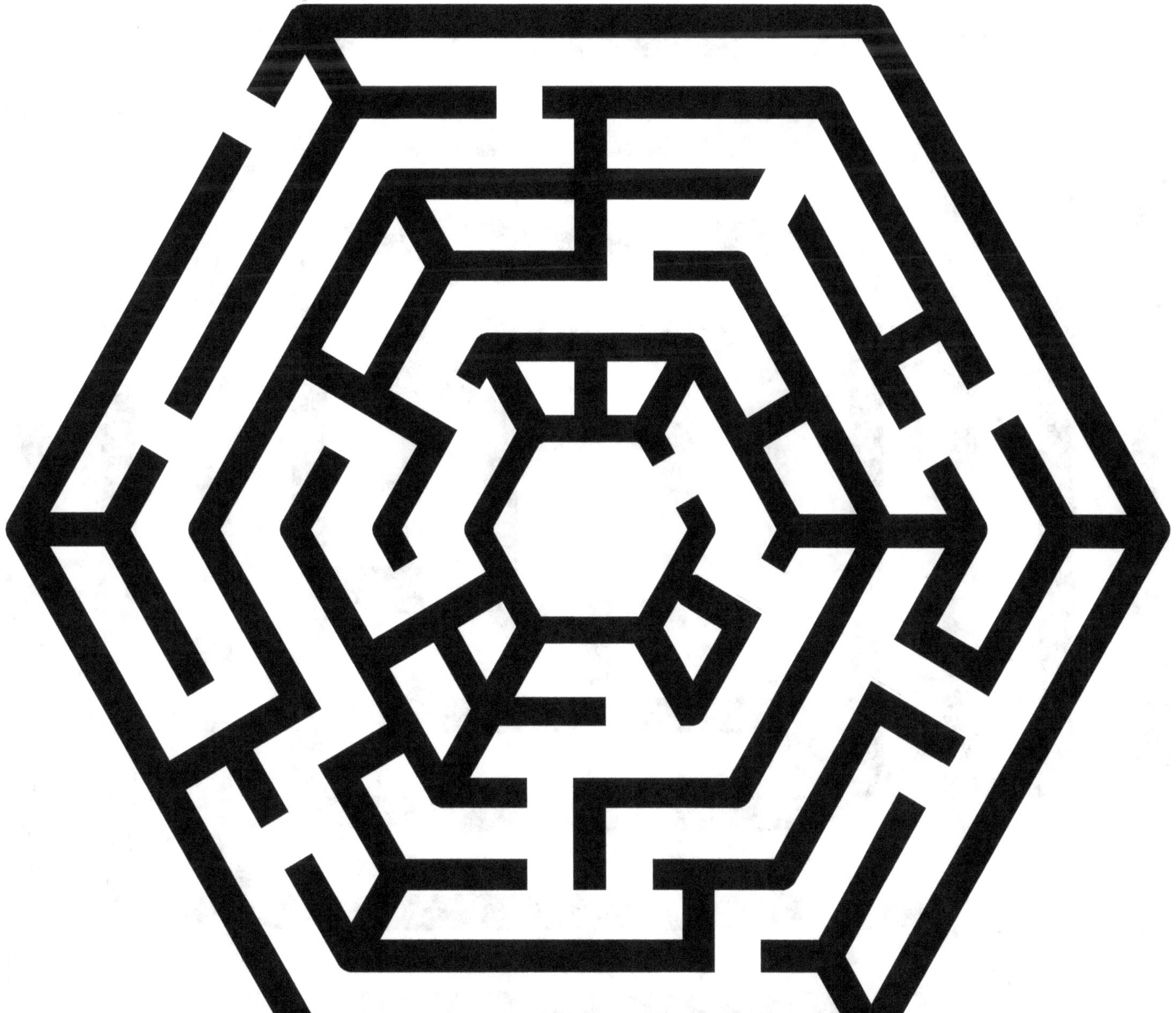

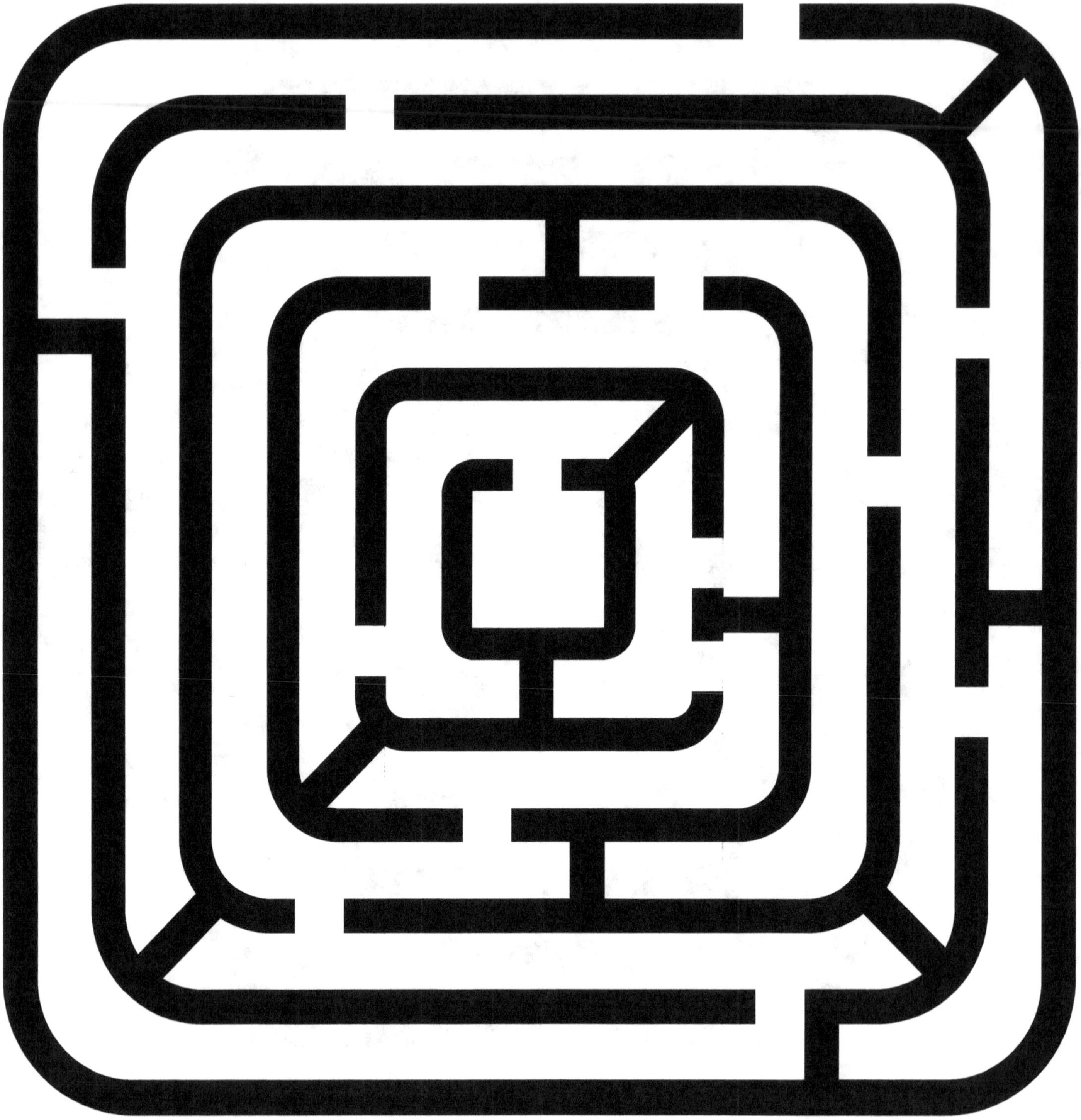

Pirate Conner's™ Sea Maze

START

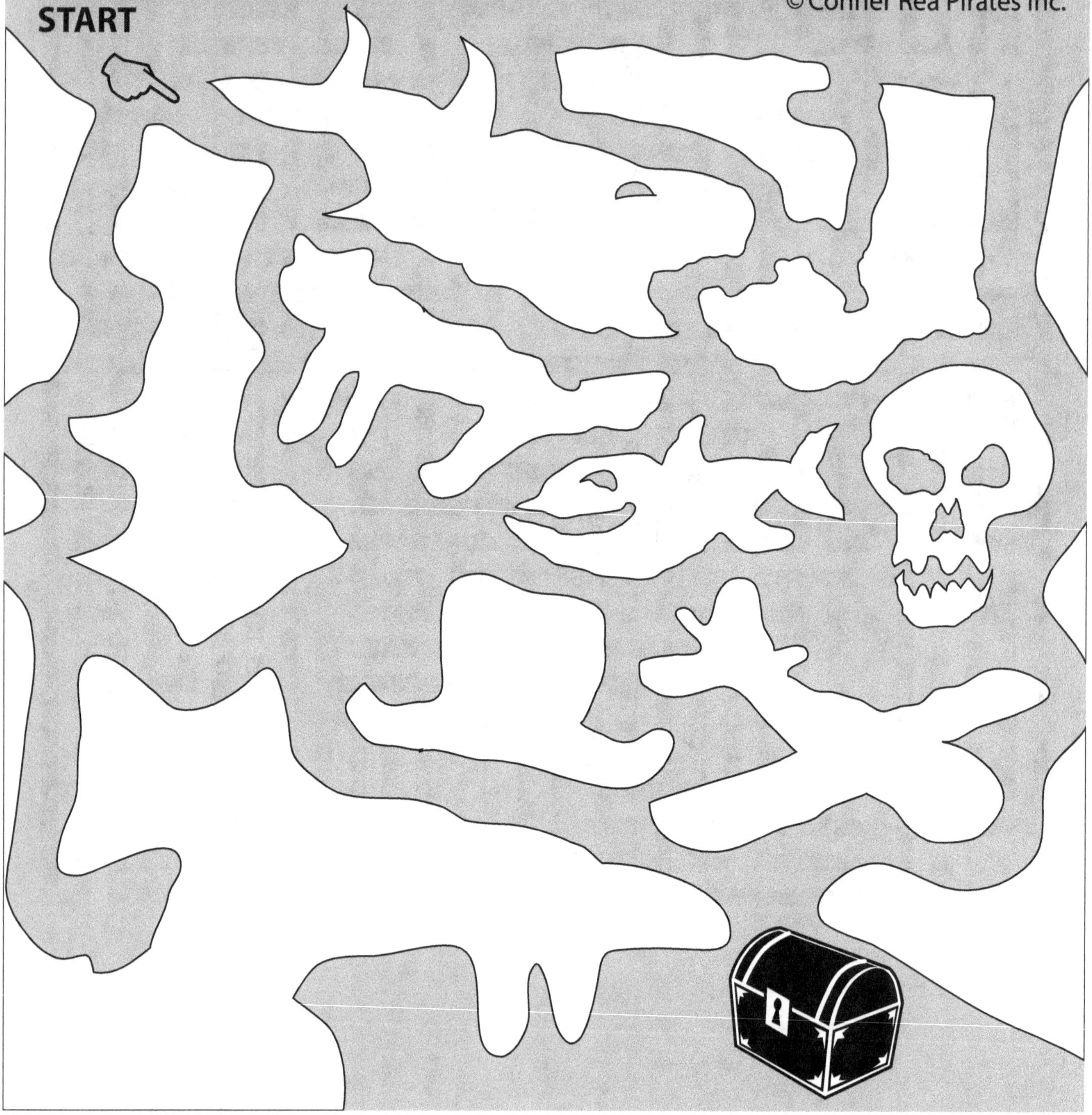

™ Pirate Conner's Sea Maze

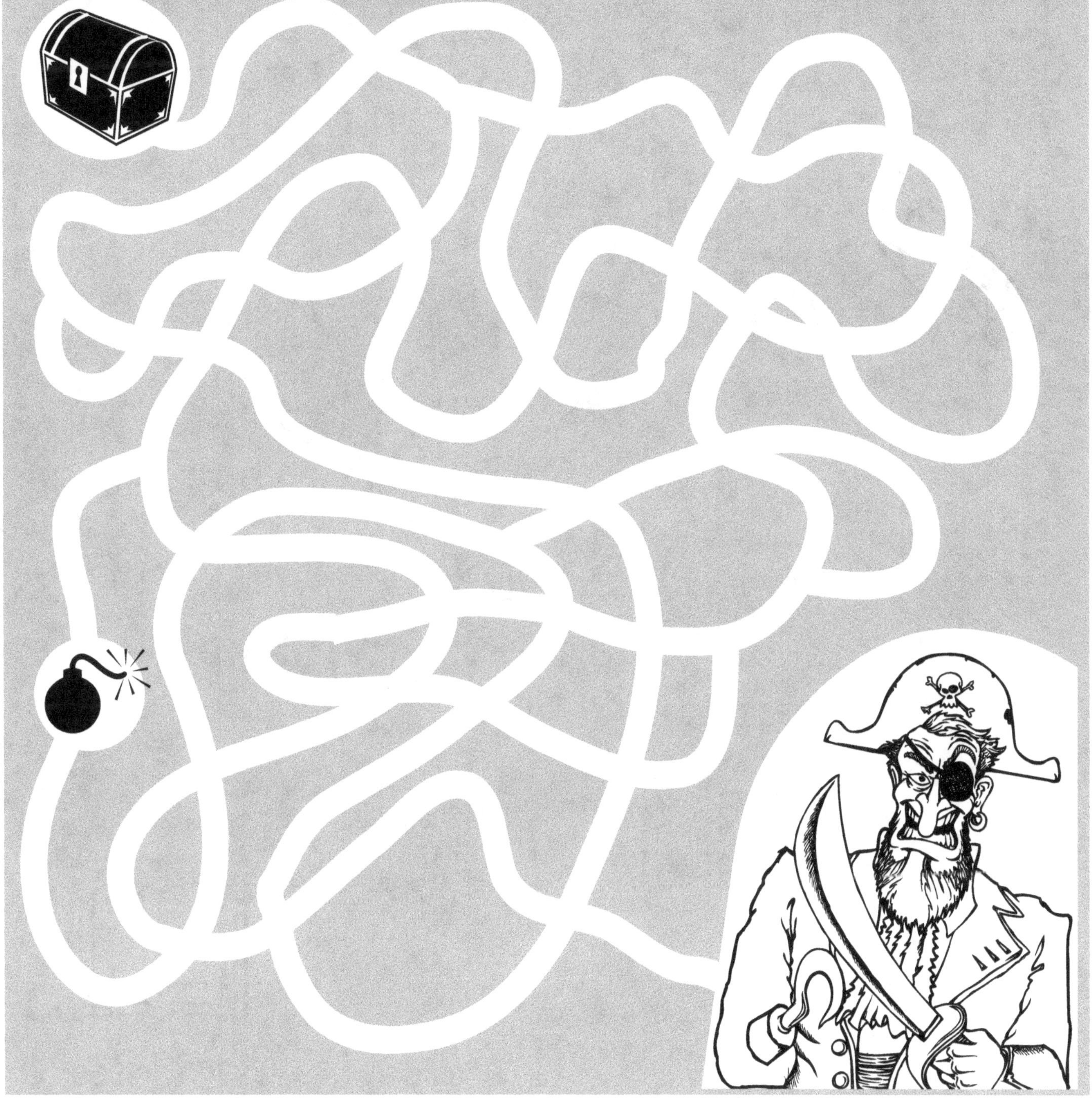

HELP TEACHER

PUT PENS TO PAPER & AVOID THE SCISSORS

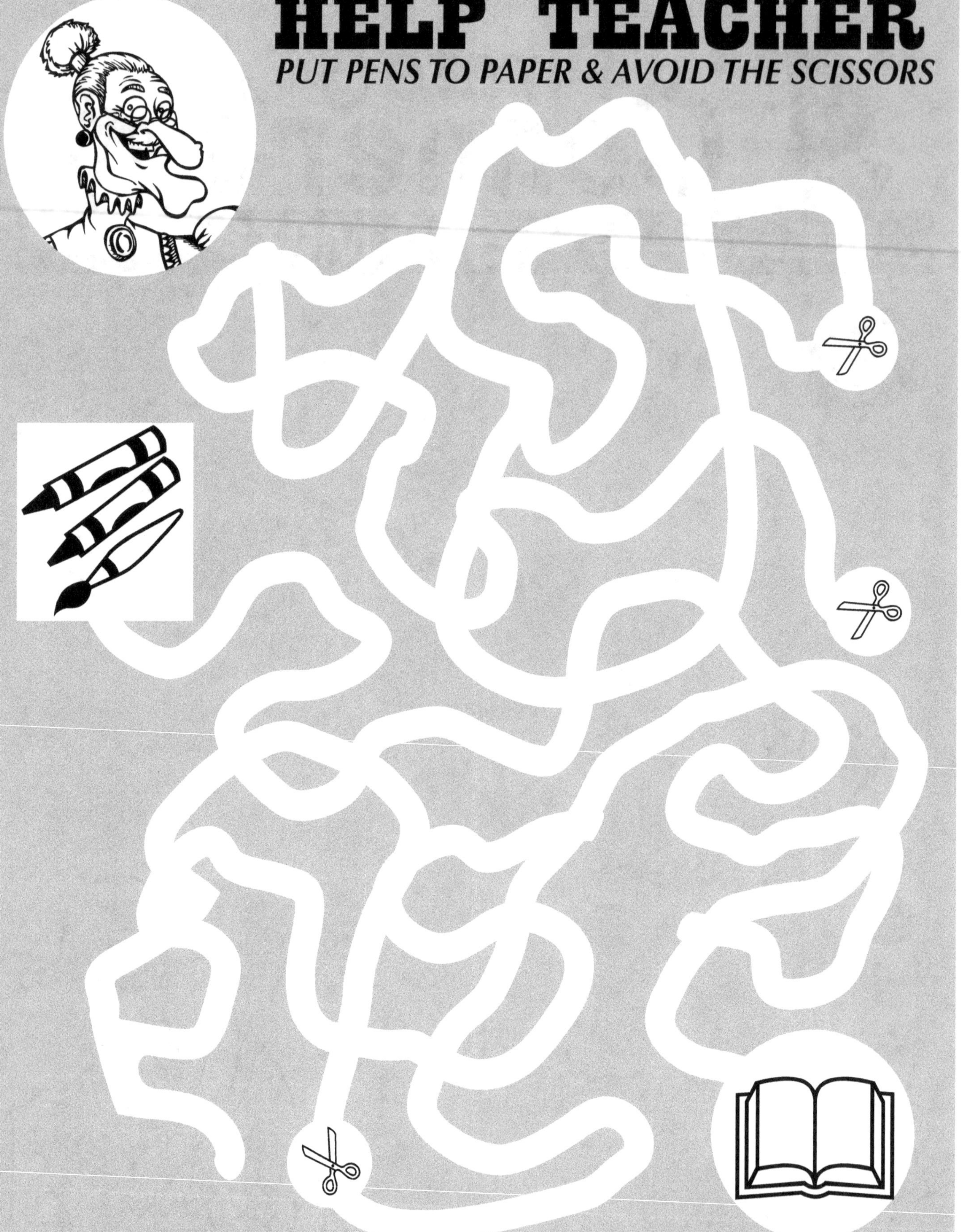

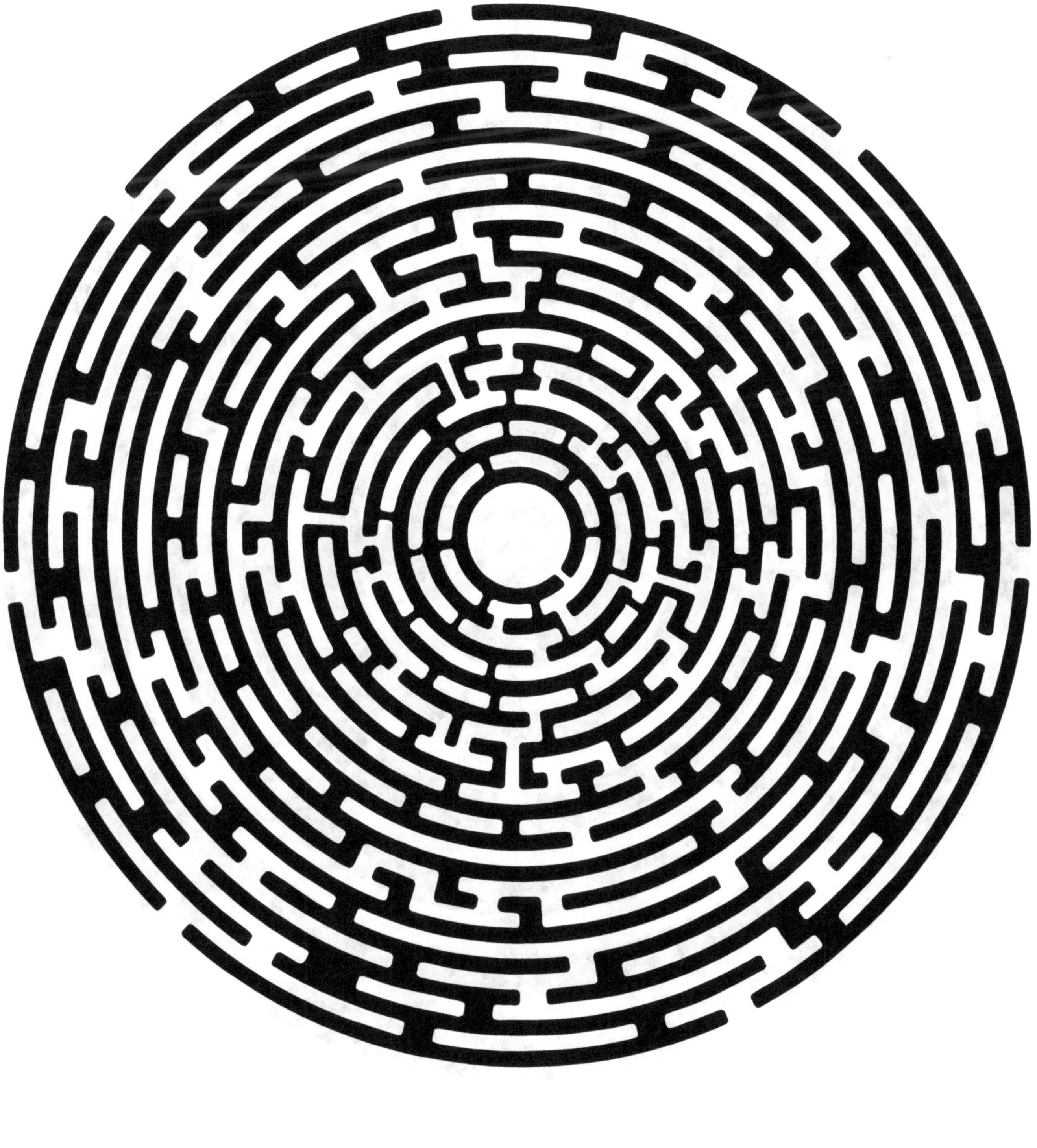

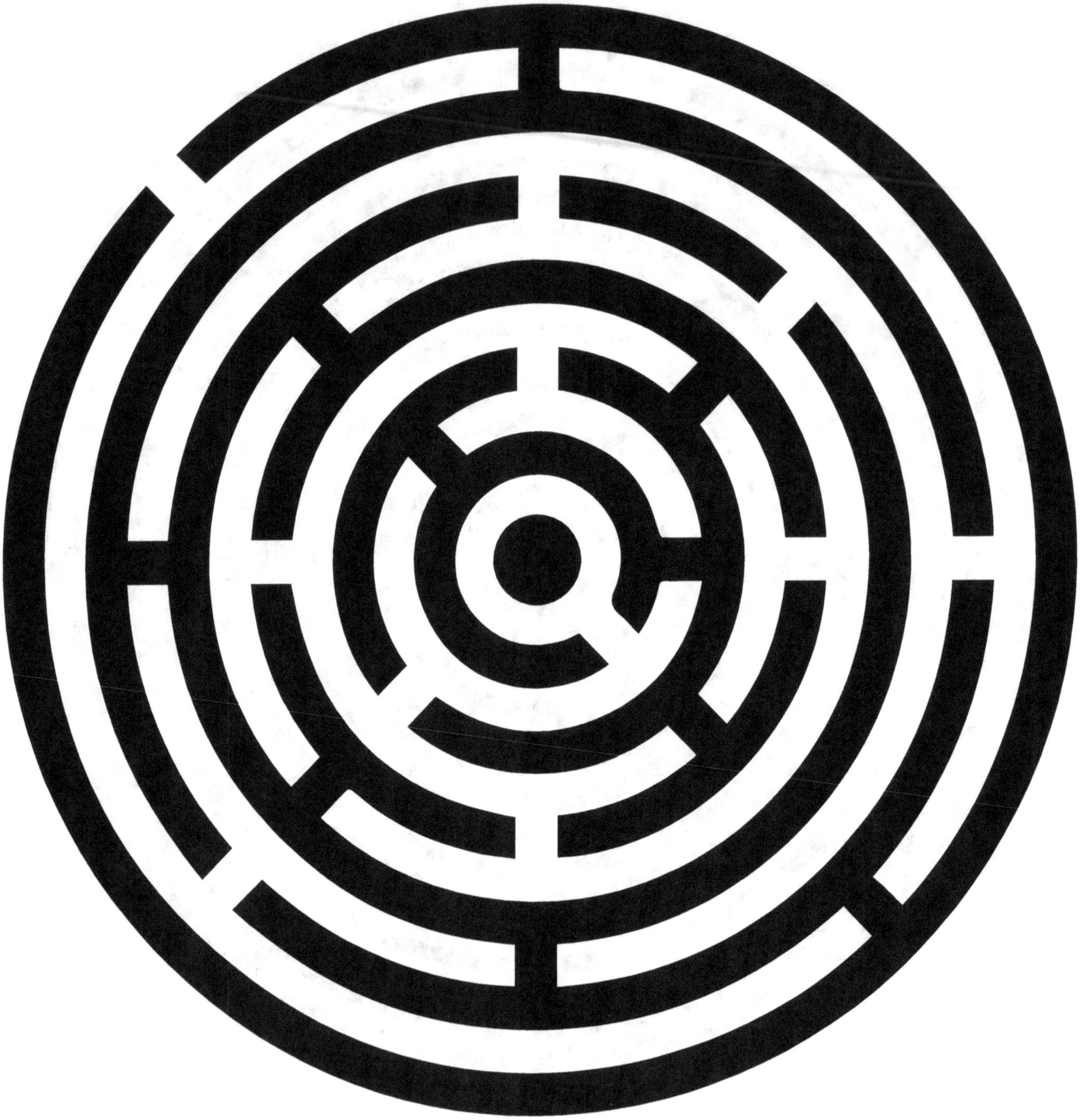

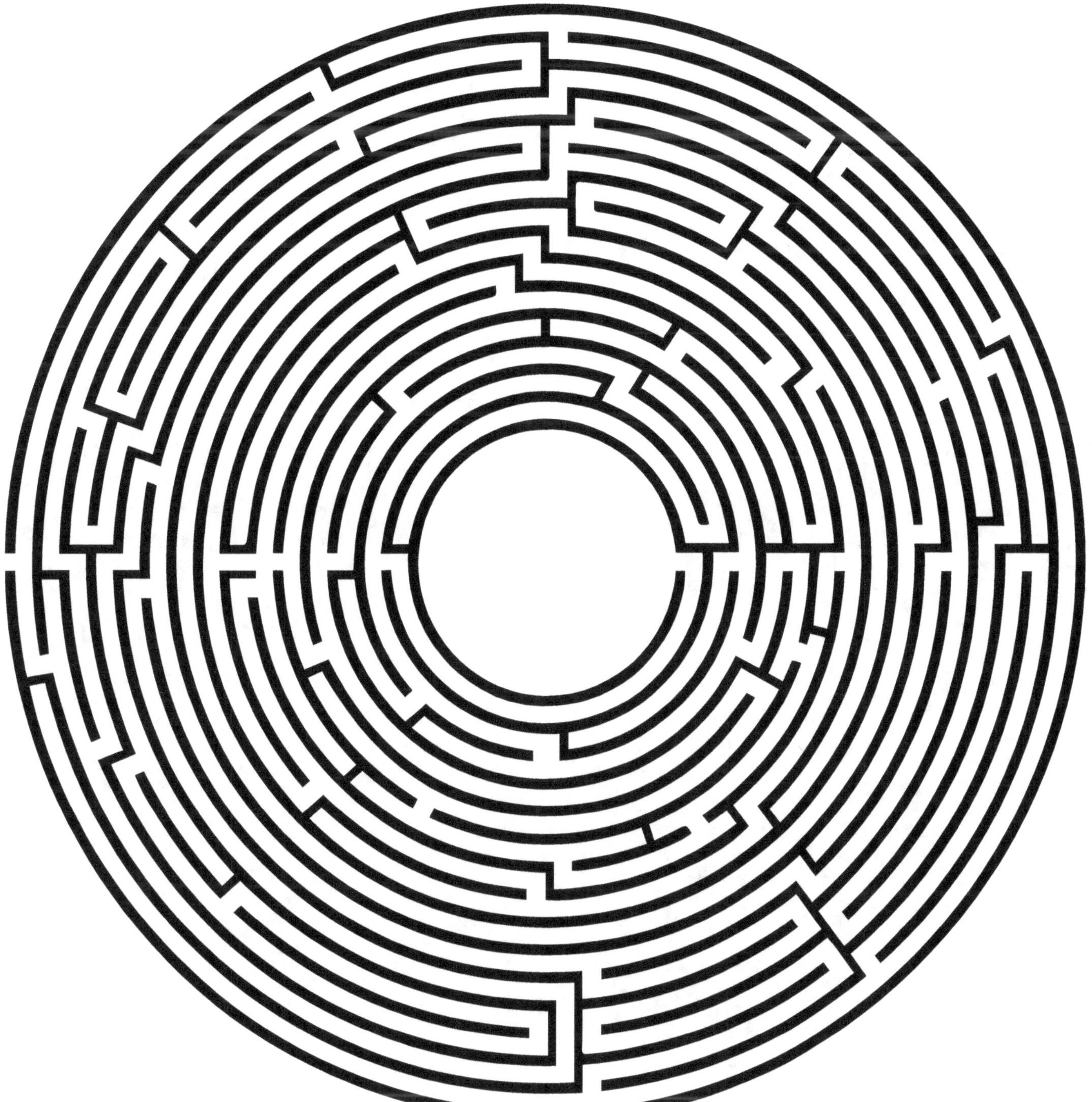

www.ingramcontent.com/pod-product-compliance
Lightning Source LLC
Chambersburg PA
CBHW080834180526
45168CB00006B/2684